Beyond Flavour

Beyond Flavour

Wine Tasting by Structure

Second Edition

Nick Jackson

Master of Wine

Cover design and illustrations by Ashton Dunn and Chloe Lombard *homo proponit, sed Deus disponit*

Table of Contents

Foreword to the Second Edition

The success of the first edition of *Beyond Flavour* was my principal pleasure in the plague year of 2020. Released at the very beginning of the year, its existence almost perfectly coincides with the Covid era. 2020 was, I suppose, a boon for book authors in a world where people suddenly had enforced time at home to read and study. Perhaps that partly explains the sales I enjoyed; some well-placed reviews helped also. But in the final analysis, what I thought were simply some idiosyncratic thoughts about wine tasting of interest to a few wine students turned out to have much broader resonance. And for that I am grateful and humbled.

Why, then, a second edition? First, to make the book more user-friendly. I took many shortcuts in the first edition because I did not anticipate a large readership. But it is appropriate now to make the book easier to read. Organisation of entries is clearer, the index helpful, the structure table a useful tool. The 'confusions' section and producer recommendations for each variety entry are meant to be of practical use. But more important than those revisions is the new content.

Since I published the first edition, I have both been invited to present on the subjects discussed in the book and have myself run webinar courses on the same. Readers are invited to view the webinar recordings on YouTube under the School of Taste channel. It is often said that you do not know a topic truly until you have taught it, and that is certainly true in this case. I became aware through many hours of teaching these subjects that some of my descriptions worked better than others; that some were confusing; that descriptions could be enhanced through the inclusion of additional material. And moreover, I developed further insights and ideas.

Two insights in particular I develop in the second edition. The first is to centralise *shape* of acid structure in white wines and *location* of tannins in red wines as being the most valuable and reliable aspects of acid and tannin structure respectively. I had mentioned in the first edition that the level and type of acidity and tannin *do* change according to climate and other factors, but perhaps I did not draw out that fact sufficiently. I emphasise that variability more in this edition, with the concomitant effect that what *does not* change – shape and location – become proportionately more important.

The second key aspect of my thought that has developed since the first edition concerns how acid, tannin and other elements of wines work together to give a distinctive taste impression. We know that acid or tannin structure contributes more than simply the skeleton or frame of a wine. It is also integral to providing attributes such as attack, texture, dryness and savouriness. But other components of a wine can do this too. What about those?

While it is good to assess structure, it is only possible to understand its full role in the context of other elements of a wine such as aromas, fruit profile, phenolic content and many others. In my conception, wine is a seesaw of different elements which need balancing against one other to realise a successful harmony. Structure is one of the most important contributing elements, but there are many others too. I try and make these others more explicit in this edition, and to that end, I have included a 'construction' summary sentence at the beginning of each variety entry; this is my attempt to summarise how the different elements of a wine work together to shape the experience of a wine on the palate.

I have always wanted to avoid the impression that the ideas I discuss in this book are tricks or 'tells' for certain wines. To reduce acid or tannin structure merely to blind tasting games does not do justice to the complex role they play in a wine. In this edition I suggest that situating structure within a broader conception of a wine's 'construction' helps explain why a wine tastes like it does, and why it behaves like it does in the mouth.

A wine is much more than a mass of fruit, acidity and tannin, but in order to get to that understanding, we do need to do the hard work of understanding the fruit, acidity and tannin. In other words, you can use this book as simply a helpful list of characteristics that different varieties and regions tend to exhibit, but you can also begin to think about how these aspects are merely stopping off points en route to a more complete and satisfying understanding of wine.

Introduction

In early July 2016, I flew from New York to Frankfurt on a red-eye flight. By noon, I was sitting in a beer garden on the southern bank of the Rhine, looking out over the expansive vineyards of the Rheingau on the steep slopes opposite. I was there for a week of visits to some of the best wine producers in Germany, followed by a week of the same in Montalcino. As I sat there, pondering the two weeks to come, I came to a realisation that would change everything about wine for me. The realisation was simple: I had been tasting wine all wrong. All wrong. It needed to change – and quickly.

A few weeks earlier, I had sat the stage one assessment (S1A) exams for the Master of Wine (MW) qualification. The purpose of the S1A is brutal but effective: to cull the wheat from the chaff of MW students. By passing, you are not awarded anything – other than the opportunity to sit the real MW exams, one year later. Progress to stage two, and you can legitimately consider yourself having a shot of becoming a Master of Wine. But failure to pass S1A means your career as a MW student never really got out of the starting blocks.

The S1A exam consists of two theory questions, each to be answered in one-hour essays, and 12 wines, tasted blind. However the questions are presented in the tasting exam, their intention is always to make the taster identify origin, variety and quality successfully. Do that, and everything else should fall into place for the rest of the questions. Now, given that the S1A exam is not meant to be as taxing as the MW exam itself, I was fairly confident I had done enough to pass the theory part. It was the tasting part that I was worried about.

A few days after the exam, I received the list of wines. I had correctly identified perhaps seven or eight out of 12 varieties, and about the same number of the countries of origin. But this was very borderline to pass. And more to the point, I had felt strongly while sitting in the exam room that ultimately I had no real justification for a lot of my answers. Even if they turned out to be right, I was more fortunate than skilled. I could not get over this nagging sense that really, too much of the time, *I was just guessing.*

I was in Germany and Italy in order to gather examples for the theory part of the exam the following year – I had booked the trip with the expectation that I would pass S1A. And even that seemed to be in doubt now. So I made up my mind while sitting there, beer in hand, that the way that I was blind tasting wines had to change. No. More. Guessing.

When I got back to New York, I learned I had, in fact, passed the S1A exam. The anonymous examiners scolded me for my less than stellar tasting, but I had scraped through. Now I had less than one year until the real exam to figure out how to taste confidently, accurately and consistently.

Flavour Folly

The way I practised blind tasting at home was simple. On a Thursday, I would buy anywhere between six and 12 wines to make a flight. Then I would taste them every day for four days, 'half blind' (I knew what the wines were, just not the order they came in). I would make each flight intentionally difficult by including wines that could easily be confused for one another.

For example, I might have a flight of: Left Bank Bordeaux, Cahors, Argentinian Malbec, Australian Shiraz, Côtes du Rhône and Bandol rouge. The first day I tasted them I would get a lot wrong. But I would note down the particular characteristics of each wine and read back my notes before the next day's session. Then I would taste again and reduce the number of mistakes.

While practice improved my tasting, it certainly did not make it perfect. In my WSET studies (qualifications earned earlier in my wine career, and necessary for entry to the MW program), I had learned to identify five different aromas and flavours present in a wine. This would surely narrow down the possibilities. But that is easier said than done, when, to use the set of wines just mentioned, any one of them could have a dominant note of blackberry.

In the flight described, another option was to consider ripeness levels. Surely Argentinian Malbec is riper than Malbec from Cahors? Of course, but then the question enters my mind, could this Argentinian Malbec actually be Argentinian Cabernet Sauvignon? As any wine student knows, though, Cabernet has a green note to it. That is the classic description. But anyone who has tasted any Left Bank cru classé Bordeaux in the past 15 years knows that Cabernet is no longer made with that green note. So both Malbec and Cabernet from a warm climate country like Argentina are full bodied, black fruited, tannic varieties. How to distinguish them?

To state the question even more acutely, here is an example of this problem that I experienced first-hand when I sat the Master of Wine exam in June 2017. The question told candidates that these two wines were made from the same predominant variety – the student's job was to identify what the variety was.

The wines were later revealed to be:

- Cuvée Juveniles, Torbreck. 2014. Barossa Valley, Australia
- Châteauneuf-du-Pape, Domaine du Vieux Lazaret. 2013. Rhône Valley, France

I clearly remember sticking my nose in both glasses, and in both, getting a distinct whiff of pepper. Sure, I tasted them thereafter, but my mind was already made up. These wines were obviously Syrah based. But no: the dominant variety was Grenache. Well, you might say, you simply mistook white for black pepper (white pepper is a classic note for Grenache, and black for Syrah). Probably I did. But can you be sure, 1) that you would never make the same mistake? and, 2) that some predominantly Grenache wines don't have a hint of black pepper, or that Syrah wines don't have a touch of white pepper?

On that question I picked up some marks, because I had identified Barossa and the Rhône Valley as the likely regions of origin. But I had walked right into the trap the examiners had set – I had not considered all the elements of the wine and had based my Syrah answer simply on flavours. From the subsequently published examiners' report, it was evident that many candidates had done the same.

When I discovered what the wines were after the exam, this mistake was particularly frustrating because I had been teaching myself not to rely on flavours for all the reasons discussed above. I was also aware that winemakers could manipulate flavour through picking date, yeast choice, blending choices, choice of ageing vessel etc. Could a variety even be trusted to taste consistently the same?

During my practice tastings in the year preceding the exam, it had become very obvious that *flavours were not helping me at all*. Anything could taste like anything. But what was the alternative to flavours? What else could you base your understanding of a wine on?

Beyond Flavour

At some point during the year leading up to the S1A exam, I had heard a MW use the expression 'acid structure' with reference to white wines. It was the first time I had heard the phrase, and it was a lightbulb moment for me. Of course, I knew that a key element of red wines was tannin structure, but now I began to consider that white wines might have a structure – a skeleton – in a similar way. I had a vague awareness that tannin structure in red wines differed between varieties, not just in terms of quantity but also in terms of quality – what the tannins felt like in the mouth. At that moment, I started wondering whether the same might be true of acid structure in white wines.

In my tastings at home, I began to focus obsessively on acid structure in whites and tannin structure in reds. I would note what the structure of different varieties felt like and amend it when I tasted wines from other producers. And then amend it again. Finally, I had a roster of structure profiles for all the major varieties. Where flavour had been an unreliable guide, I found that the structure of a variety changes far less, whatever the winemaker or climate does. And without even realising it was happening, I started getting a lot more wines correct. And more importantly, I was not guessing any longer.

When the exam came around, I had been focusing on structure for months. And on paper 1 – the white wines paper – I relied on it in a striking way. One of the wines on the paper was clearly European by its dryness and overall balance, but it was simply covered in new French oak to the exclusion of all other aromas. There was nothing to smell here, other than winemaking. If you are invested in a flavour-led approach, how do you approach a wine like that?

I got stuck on the wine and was spending too long on it (the MW tasting exams are a rush – you absolutely must maintain your discipline to ensure you finish every question). I wrote out the answer for a white Rioja, one of a handful of European white wines that can see a lot of oak. But it just did not feel right. There was a firm acidity at the heart of the wine, but it was well masked by a rich, slightly viscous texture and high alcohol. I scratched my white Rioja answer and wrote a Condrieu answer. After the exam, I was the only person I spoke to who got the wine right.* Relying on structure had been the key. I felt vindicated.

Ignoring flavour, I passed the MW theory and tasting exams at the first attempt in June 2017 and became a Master of Wine in February 2019.

———————————————

This book is an attempt to describe key characteristics of the major grape varieties and wine-producing regions to facilitate wine identification and improve understanding. My methodology relies on assessing a wine's structure first and foremost: that is, how the wine *feels* in the mouth. That is why I dedicate a substantial section at the beginning of the book to explaining a structure-based approach to tasting.

However, while many grape varieties can be identified using structure alone, supporting evidence is invaluable to confirm an identification. Whatever can help with the difficult task of identifying wines I have pushed into service in the descriptions of varieties that follow, foremost among which is my attempt to describe the overall sensation of a wine through the 'construction' sentence at the beginning of each variety entry. While the following pages do not focus *solely* on structure, structure remains the golden thread throughout.

Finally, a word of warning: all my perceptions are just that — mine. The way I try to explain a wine's principal characteristics may not resonate with you. In that case, ignore whatever does not speak to you. But in the time since I passed the exam, I have taught my approach to many students, and not one has failed to tell me that it has helped them. My wish is that it may help you, too.

*The wine was: Condrieu, Côteau de Vernon, Georges Vernay, 2014. I subsequently tasted this wine, and it is not at all oaky – it was a strange showing.

How to Use this Book

The purpose of this book is to improve your understanding of important wine varieties, regions and styles. If you are a wine lover, you should learn a lot about what makes wines taste as they do. If you are a wine student facing blind tasting exams, it should directly help your blind tasting skills. In the grape variety entries, I discuss all attributes I think most helpful to facilitate correct wine identifications.

To that end, you should use the book in whatever way best meets your needs. Certainly, you do not have to read the book all the way through. It is a reference book, to come back to as you are tasting. There is only one essential section to read, and that is the following one, about the structure-based approach. You have to read that in order to understand my approach and my terminology throughout. You may also wish to read the introduction to Tasting for Grape Variety, which explains in more detail the components of each grape variety entry.

The main part of the book is a study of the different varieties. I work through 59 important wine grape varieties and discuss the characteristics I find most distinctive for each, including, but not limited to, structure. In addition, I describe the characteristics of key regional styles for each grape variety. That is, under Pinot Noir, I describe what wines from the most important appellations of red Burgundy taste like. Of necessity, I could only include the most important regions, those commonly found on international markets.

I then move on to separate entries for sparkling, sweet, fortified, rosé and orange wines. Rather than treat these under their grape varieties, I thought it preferable to separate them out and focus on the style of the wines, simply because the style of these wines usually speaks louder than the varieties that go into them. But it goes without saying that the influence of the varieties is still strong, so each entry should be read in conjunction with that of the relevant variety/ies.

Later in the book, I discuss some general considerations of tasting for origin. That is, what characteristics of a wine tell you about where its grape are grown? I look first at how to taste for climate, and then examine key wine producing countries. Here, the emphasis is less on structure (because I have largely covered that under the section on grape varieties) and more on general characteristics typical of wines from each country.

Please note that when it comes to grape varieties, I focus *on the most important varieties worldwide.* Since much of the readership of this book will be those studying wine, I focus on the varieties which it is fair to expect students to have some experience of. Are there sometimes unusual varieties on wine exams? Of course, but in that case, questions are more likely to focus on identifying origin and on wine style than on identifying the variety. So if you are particularly interested in varieties grown in Jura, Croatia or many other regions, you will need to refer to more detailed texts for your information.

At the end of the book, I address one of wine tasting's most fundamental but least well performed tasks: tasting for quality. For professional purposes, the ability to assess quality is far more important than being able to identify variety or origin – and yet we often seem to neglect it.

Throughout the book, I use technical language beyond just that associated with wine structure. I have tried to define the more technical wine terms in the Tasting Glossary.

A Word of Caution

In his book *Range*, David Epstein draws a contrast between 'conceptual' and 'procedural' problems (2019, pp. 82ff). Procedural problems simply require the outworking of a learned method to arrive at a solution. Conceptual problems are ones which '[connect] students to a broader concept, rather than just a procedure.' Procedural problems are more quickly executed once the method is understood, but less likely to cause the student to engage with any broader conceptual implications. Conceptual problems, meanwhile, are taxing and often complicated, but ultimately teach the student how to think through a problem, rather than just execute a solution.

This book discusses the conceptual problem of how best to taste wine in order to understand it. I develop a methodology in response, one that requires rigorous engagement when tasting and which must be carefully applied every time. Since I am proposing a method (a 'concept') of wine tasting, I have to put it to the test, which is what the entries on the grape varieties are. And that always risks the entries looking as if they are the 'final word' on the grape variety in question (incidentally, the table of structure risks that even more, but I had so many requests for it I felt obliged to include it). It also risks encouraging readers simply to roll out a 'procedural' response: if this is the wine, the correct language to describe it is x, y, z.

Indeed, the most common misreading of the first edition was to interpret the book as a kind of 'da Vinci code' of wine tasting which, since I had 'cracked' it, all that readers needed to do was memorise my language and repeat as needed. I dislike this reading of the book. While I understand why it happened (and that I am probably at fault for it), the book is much better read as a *conceptual proposal for a method of tasting* rather than any definitive judgement on what wines taste like — which will never be reached as long as there are human beings tasting wine.

I would be most satisfied if readers would focus on the *method* rather than on the *results* that I have suggested. Use the method and you may come up with different results, but you will have improved your wine tasting skills.

A word on generalisations

A book like this requires drawing detailed and specific conclusions from a broad mass of data – in this case, the many wines I have tasted over years of study and teaching. While I am confident in the profiles for varieties presented here, when it comes to their regional identities, I have had to use a necessarily broad brushstroke.

Due to the diversity of wine styles in any wine region, any generalisation will have exceptions – in fact, numerous ones. But I maintain a belief that regional characteristics do exist. My simple supporting evidence: the fact that people like me have passed blind tasting exams which ask about these characteristics. Using the general descriptions included in these pages, I have successfully identified many regions in blind tastings.

Nonetheless, you should *expect* to find examples that do not conform to my descriptions, both because my descriptions are far from perfect, and because of the numerous stylistically divergent wines. Wine regions and styles are changing so quickly it is difficult to keep up; I have simply made my best attempt here.

The website

The first edition of the book featured a vintage guide for important fine wine producing regions. I have now housed this on my website: vintagevariation.com/beyond-flavour so I can update it annually.

On that page you will also find **downloadable PDFs** of the table of structure (Appendix II) and the table of indicative analytical values (Appendix III).

A few disclaimers

The approach to tasting I describe in this book is a *sensory* one. That is, it is based on what our senses tell us as we taste. It certainly is not a scientific approach. I would be very happy if someone discovered scientific evidence for the suggestions I make about structure, but I certainly do not claim any scientific authority.

I have already mentioned my mistrust of flavours, and I am aware that this stands in contrast to many, if not most, approaches to tasting. However, you will note that I *do* talk about flavours. I try, though, to confine them as much as possible to *confirmatory evidence* once an initial identification has been formed on the basis of some other more reliable element, often structure.

You will also notice that, in contrast to many tasting processes/grids, I do not linger on wine colour. Where it is particularly noteworthy (for example, if it is particularly deep or pale), of course it is appropriate to mention it as confirmatory evidence. But with a few obvious exceptions, colour has never done much for me other than eliminate some possibilities.

One important consideration as you are tasting for variety: higher-priced wines will tend to show varietal characteristics more clearly than cheaper examples. More careful winemaking from higher quality regions of origin allow a variety to express itself most clearly. Wines priced under USD/EUR 12 or GBP 10 may not, therefore, be the best examples to work with as you read through the entries on each variety. Above that price, you should begin to perceive variety increasingly clearly. So read the next section, then dip into the entries on your favourite varieties or wine styles – glass in hand, naturally.

Jupiter, Florida, Feast of the Assumption, 2022

Structure: The Basics

Acid Structure in White Wines

While acidity often goes unmentioned in red wines, in white wines, it is a central element that any taster must consider. And yet there is often far more to acidity in whites than many tasters realise.

In the simplest terms, acid is a white wine's structure, its skeleton, while the fruit is the flesh. Acid structure is intrinsic to white varieties in the same way that tannin structure is to reds. In both cases, you assess structure on the palate. Each variety has a slightly different acid structure, so if you can perceive the structure correctly, you should be able to identify the variety.

So how do you perceive acid structure in white wines?

There are three key elements to acid structure. They are: shape, type and level of acidity. All three should be tasted while the wine is in your mouth, before swallowing/spitting, although the finish of the wine may be used to confirm your impressions.

I will explain each below, beginning with the most important: the shape of acidity. While type and level can change according to climate and winemaking, shape is the most consistent and reliable and for that reason the most important to start with.

Shape of acidity

The most difficult – but ultimately most valuable – of all the ways of assessing a white wine's acidity is to consider what *shape* the acid structure assumes on the palate. Every major variety has a slightly different shape of acidity in the mouth: if you can perceive it correctly, it will much improve your understanding of the variety.

So what does it mean to say that acidity has a shape? In very simple terms, acidity is felt in different places and at different levels during the journey of the wine across the palate. By 'journey' I mean *the period the wine spends in your mouth*. Acidity may be felt primarily on entry. Or on the finish. Or both. And if felt on both start and finish, it may remain consistent in terms of its level, or it may increase or decrease between the two. By combining where the acidity is felt (beginning, middle, end) with how strongly it is felt at these points, you can identify a 'shape' to each acid structure.

Using the example of Chenin Blanc, Chenin has a *crescendo* shaped acid structure. That is, on entry the wine feels quite soft, without much obvious acidity. But as you hold the wine on the palate, the acidity seems to increase, until it really screams on the finish. It grows, or crescendos, from start to finish.

Chenin Blanc in fact has one of the more interesting shapes of acidity: others are more uniform (e.g. Chardonnay, Semillon). But every variety has a shape to the acidity; the task is to learn what they are and be able to identify them.

Type of acidity

Correctly identifying the shape of acidity narrows down your range of possible grape varieties. But a helpful technique to home in further is to assess the *type* of acidity. By 'type' I mean *the quality* of the acidity – what it feels like.

To continue with the same example, classic Loire Chenin Blanc has a *bracing* quality to the acidity. That is, you feel that the enamel on your teeth is in danger if you keep the wine in your mouth too long. The acidity is so strong, it really wakes you up. By contrast, Riesling (another highly acidic variety) has a different *type* of acidity, which results in a totally different, more tingling and less piercing sensation on the palate.

The type of acidity can, frustratingly, be affected by factors such as climate, yield and winemaking. So as with level of acidity (below) we can only speak with qualified confidence about the type of each major variety's acidity. In my descriptions in this book, I have tried to identify the *most common* types of acidity for each variety.

I will describe the different types of acidity of each major white variety in the sections dedicated to each. But to persist with the example of Chenin Blanc, when combining the first two of our three categories for assessing acid structure, we can now say that Chenin Blanc has 'crescendo shaped, bracing acidity'. That already is a very detailed description. But through our final technique – assessing the *level* of the acidity – we can make this description even more specific to the variety.

One note of caution: I have a preferred term for each variety's type of acidity ('bracing' in the case of Chenin or 'jagged' for Sauvignon Blanc). You may have a different term that more accurately captures the quality of the acidity. Use whatever term speaks to you but ensure that it is one that will also be understood by others.

Level of acidity

This is usually the simplest of the three elements to identify. How much acidity is there in this wine? This category comes last in our assessment of the three components of acid structure because the answer for any variety can be heavily dependent on the growing climate or even the vintage conditions. But *in the most general terms* some varieties have more acidity than others. If something smells like a Sauvignon Blanc but has low acidity, it is unlikely to be a Sauvignon Blanc. Sauvignon Blanc without acidity would be pointless.

Here are a few broad categories:

High acidity: Riesling, Sauvignon Blanc, Albariño, Chenin Blanc, Aligoté, Furmint

Moderate acidity: Chardonnay, Pinot Gris, Marsanne, Viura, Viognier, Arneis, Verdicchio

Low acidity: Gewürztraminer

Tip: in contrast to what most tasters intuitively believe, very few white varieties actually have low acidity. Usually they just have moderate *but soft* acidity.

How do you perceive level of acidity? The best way is the classic way: how much does this wine make you salivate? If you are still hesitant about answering that question, after you have swallowed/spat, leave your mouth open for 5-10 seconds, and you will have your answer. The more your mouth waters, the higher the level of acidity.

Another test is to line up three glasses, non-blind, and taste in order: from a Gewürtztraminer, to a Chardonnay and finally a Loire Chenin Blanc, to see the movement from low to high acidity.

So now we can put together the three strands of acid structure analysis: shape, type and level. If we encountered a Chenin Blanc, we could say that it has: 'a crescendo shaped acid structure, with a high level of bracing acidity'. And with a description that tight, you are only left with one option for variety.

Again, type and level of acidity vary at least somewhat according to factors such as region of origin, yields and winemaking decisions. It is possible to say that Chardonnay has moderate levels of acidity, and that statement is often true. But it is clearly not true in Champagne. Or that Riesling has steely acidity; almost always true, but in Austria it can often be more tangy. Understanding the limitations of level and type of acidity means that while we can make general comments on those, you should expect to find differences within them across different wines and regions.

All of this goes to show the key importance of the *shape* of acidity. For my contention is that whatever style of wine or region or winemaking, the elemental shape of a white wine's acidity does not change. For that reason, of the three elements of acid structure, shape is the most important for understanding a wine's structure.

In many respects, this is a frustrating aspect of a structural approach to tasting white wines, because the concept of the shape of acidity is a hard one to grasp immediately, and also because even if you do, tasting for shape is difficult. However, acid shape remains the most reliable indicator of a variety's identity and with attentive tasting, most wine tasters will soon understand it.

If you are also identifying a wine's region of origin, identifying the variety correctly reduces the range of possible regions of origin to those where the variety is cultivated. At this point, an analysis of how ripe the wine is and in what style it has been made will provide the best evidence for where the wine comes from. I discuss how to perform this analysis in Tasting for Region of Origin.

Tannin Structure in Red Wines

Tannin structure in red wines is a far more familiar concept than acid structure in whites. But again, while familiarity with the idea is strong, the full potential of tannin structure as a tool for identifying varieties remains underappreciated. For acid structure in white wines, we discussed shape, type and level of acidity. For tannin structure in red wines, two of those categories remain, and one changes. The three components of tannin structure are: location of tannin, type of tannin and level of tannin.

These three elements of tannin structure are best tasted *on the finish of the wine*; i.e., after you have swallowed or spat. Listen to what the tannins are telling you at that point; they will not reveal all their secrets while the wine is in your mouth. Let us examine each of these three components in turn.

Location of tannin

The tannins for each different red variety are perceived in different physical places in your mouth. If you have never really thought about *where* you feel tannins, you would probably imagine that on the palate, tannins are felt all over. But more careful tasting will reveal otherwise.

To use the example of Sangiovese, the tannins are felt on the gums, rather than on the tongue or in the cheeks. Does this mean that there is no sensation of drying whatsoever on the tongue or in the cheeks? No, of course not. It means that in general, *the focus of the drying effects* of the tannins is felt on the gums.

The shape of a white wine's acid structure is the most difficult but also the most useful way to assess a white wine. In the same vein, learning to identify *where* in your mouth you feel a red wine's tannins may be tricky, but can hugely facilitate identification.

Now, there are a large number of varieties where the tannins are felt on the gums. By itself, that information is useless. But when combined with assessments of level and of type of tannin, it is possible to identify the variety much more easily.

Type of tannin

Just as white wines have different types of acidity, so red wines have different types, or textures, of tannin. To use one example, Sangiovese has *sandy* tannins. The tannins feel a little like rubbing your palate with sandpaper. Other types of tannin are a bit more amorphous: 'loose knit' or 'fine grained' are perhaps less easy to understand readily. That terminology does not describe the texture as clearly as 'sandy' does. I will discuss each type of tannin and how to identify and understand it under the relevant section for each variety. Once again though, describing a Chianti Classico as having 'sandy tannins felt on the gums' is a much more effective description than simply saying 'tannins felt on the gums.'

A final note. All the descriptions in this book are written on the assumption that you are tasting the wine 1-3 years after bottling, when wines are usually commercially available. During bottle ageing, the process of tannin polymerisation (small molecules of tannins combining to form longer chains) has the effect of creating a *softer type or texture of tannin*. A wine that has particularly grainy or sandy tannin will never lose it completely, but polymerisation will make the tannins feel smoother. If you are tasting an older red wine (perceived by the presence of tertiary aromas and flavours), be aware that the tannins will taste smoother and softer than my descriptions may suggest.

Level of tannin

This is the most readily understandable of the three components of tannin structure. Different varieties show different levels of tannin. Once again, this will depend on a range of factors including climate of origin, age of the wine and winemaking style. But *in general,* we can suggest the following tannin levels for some major varieties:

High: Cabernet Sauvignon, Nebbiolo, Aglianico, Malbec

Moderate: Merlot, Tempranillo, Sangiovese, Grenache, Cabernet Franc, Syrah

Tip: while varieties like Pinot Noir, Gamay or Corvina *can* have low levels of tannin, in this book, I put them all in the moderate category since so many examples have at least moderate levels (think Central Otago, Brouilly and Amarone, respectively).

Correctly assessing the tannin level is an excellent clue to what the variety might be. The easiest way of doing this is simply to consider how much the tannins dry out your mouth. The more they do, and the quicker they do (while you hold the wine in your mouth), the higher the level of tannin the variety has.

Many Argentinian Malbec wines, for example, will start creating a drying session almost immediately upon entry. Young grand cru red Burgundy, by contrast, will dry out your mouth – but only after 10 or more seconds on the palate.

That final point is also a reminder that if you hold almost any red wine on the palate for an extended length of time, it will seem quite tannic. Avoid drying out your palate by standardising the amount of time you spend with the wine on your palate to, say, five seconds or fewer.

In the case of Sangiovese, 'moderate to high levels of sandy tannins, felt on the gums', quickly reduces the number of possibilities. From there, it is possible to deduce the origin of the wine through analysis of other attributes: fruit concentration, fruit texture, acidity, length, etc.

At this point, it is necessary to submit the same qualification as that stated above in connection with white wines. Both level and type of tannin will be dependent on variable factors, and, as such, can change. That is, a winemaker may choose to extract more or less tannins during fermentation, thus rendering difficult a straightforward association between a variety and the level of tannins it should exhibit. And when it comes to type of tannin, it is simply a fact that warmer climates (or vintages) show a different type of tannin to that of the same variety grown in a cooler climate (see, for example, the entry on Syrah).

All of which is to say that the *location* of tannins is, like the shape of acidity for white wines, the most constant, reliable and important feature of assessing tannin structure in red wines. Whatever the climate or winemaking, the location of the tannins in the mouth remains the same variety by variety.

Annoyingly, this does not help the taster very much because there are simply *not that many* places in your mouth where you can feel the tannins. Your options are rather limited (unlike the shape of acidity, where your imagination is your guide). So you will see in the descriptions of each variety below, and in the table of structure, considerable repetition of location. Almost all Italian red varieties show tannins on the gums, as do all the Bordeaux varieties. That is a lot of varieties! But once again, the key is to combine this knowledge of location of tannins with level and type of tannins to arrive at a logical conclusion.

Analysing wines through the lens of acid and tannin structure requires a kind of rewiring of your brain if you have been focused for a long time on flavours. But in my experience, the reward will be far greater consistency in tasting, and stronger justifications for your identifications. It is not easy, but if you want to improve your tasting and acquire a deeper understanding of how varieties work in the glass, it is well worth the challenge.

Tasting Glossary

A lot of the descriptions below focus on tasting distinct elements of a wine and their interplay. So it useful to define some of the terms used in this book, whether they derive from the grapes or from winemaking techniques. Note that aspects related to the production of sweet, fortified and sparkling wines are handled in those sections, not here.

Acid structure consists of shape, type and level of acidity, as described in the entries on white grape varieties.

Acid structure in red wines is a difficult thing to taste for, because the density of the fruit and tannins can obscure acidity. However, in the entries on red varieties, I have done my best to articulate any particularly notable acid structures in red wines. Where there is no comment, you should assume that the acid structure is not particularly prominent or influential in determining the feel of the wine in the mouth.

Acidification in a wine (the addition of acidity to the must at fermentation due to lower than desired natural levels) is perceptible by an unexpected freshness of acidity on the finish of a ripe wine, and through a certain hardness of texture, given by low pH. Acidified wines are perhaps best identified by the sense of the acidity being out of place: after rich, ripe, soft fruit a sudden fresh acidity appears. It doesn't feel natural, and it probably isn't!

Back palate wines are those which seem to come alive on the finish. The focal point of interest and complexity is at the end. An example would be an Italian white variety such as Garganega or Verdicchio, which may not offer considerable fruit at the beginning, but can show subtle aromatic complexity and interest on the finish. By contrast, many more fruity wines show their charms as soon as you put the wine in your mouth: the interest is at the front/beginning.

Carbonic maceration makes simple, fruity wines with little structure. This renders them difficult to study using the method outlined in this book. I would contend that they are also very difficult to assess using a flavour/aroma approach, since they express more of their winemaking process (banana, bubble gum aromas) than they do of the variety. Not tasting like their variety and not having the structure of their variety ensures that for study purposes, carbonically macerated wines are challenging!

Some winemakers use a proportion of carbonically macerated fruit to provide a touch of vibrant fruitiness to otherwise conventionally made wines.

Fruit is felt on the middle of the tongue and can almost seem to 'weigh down' the tongue. I use the middle of the tongue and '**mid palate**' almost interchangeably.

Use of malolactic fermentation, lees and bâtonnage are winemaking techniques which give texture. All of them are perceived in the same location as the fruit: the tongue.

Malolactic fermentation softens acidity and gives an overall softer texture to the wine, although it is extremely difficult to be absolutely confident about its usage because the level of malic acid to be converted may be very low in the first place, resulting in little change in the finished wine. It does not change the shape of the acidity.

The use of **lees** (dead yeast cells) gives a light, soapy texture in the mid palate; not enough to be called creamy, but certainly a richer texture than the fruit alone would supply in wines like Muscadet. **Bâtonnage** gives the most generously rich, creamy texture to the mid palate of these three winemaking techniques, so much so that it can even create a sense of experiencing some thickness or solids on the tongue.

Micro-oxygenation is a winemaking technique which involves bubbling tiny amounts of oxygen through a wine prior to bottling. The main purpose is to soften tannins, particularly in powerful red varieties such as Tannat. It is a process designed to make the wine more approachable when young. For our purposes, it is very difficult to assert with absolute confidence that a wine has been subject to 'micro-ox,' so to assess the effects of the process on tannin structure may seem a bit redundant. However, just as tannins soften with age, so too do tannins subject to micro-ox.

Maybe the best advice is simply to look out for wines whose tannins feel softer than you expect them to be. Just as with an acidified wine (see acidification, above), when the wine features a surprise in one of its components, stop for a moment to consider why it may be.

Mid palate refers both to the 'middle' of the mouth – the tongue – and to the 'middle' of the tasting experience. Fruit is felt particularly strongly during the middle of the time the wine spends on your palate. While of course it is tasted right from the beginning of the tasting experience all the way through the finish, the focal point for experiencing fruit is the middle of that period.

Oak tannins are tasted on the gums. Oak tannins may be perceived by a slight grainy, woody hardness, or even, in bad examples, a sensation of wood splinters hitting the gums. They are more rigid and do not share the same suppleness as grape tannins.

pH in wine is correlated with how strongly we perceive acidity. Low pH levels usually leave wines feeling fresh and vibrant, while high pH wines feel softer (as one example, Riesling usually has low pH, Gewürztraminer, high pH). Usually, but not always, low pH and high acidity go together, and vice versa.

Phenolics in white wines play a similar role to tannins in red wines: they give a drying sensation and contribute a sense of structure. Phenolics are most commonly experienced on the gums and on the finish, where they give a chewy, pithy texture and sometimes a touch of bitterness. They contribute to sapidity (see below).

Residual sugar is tasted on the tip of the tongue. For advice on how to estimate the level of residual sugar, see Sweet Wine.

Sapidity is the experience of savouriness in the mouth. It is a useful term that I employ occasionally, because it encompasses more than simply 'acidity' or 'freshness'. Jean-Baptiste Lécaillon, winemaker at Champagne Louis Roederer, has noted that sapidity can include aspects as diverse as acidity, salinity, phenolics and minerality. In other words, sapidity covers any non-fruit elements of a wine that contribute to a savoury sensation in the mouth. Since tannins are usually the obvious savoury component of red wines, sapidity is usually discussed in the context of white or rosé wines.

In white wines that lack acidity, phenolics or salinity may add a sense of savoury bite or attack, which compensates for the low acidity. Or, in wines like Assyrtiko or Albariño, all these elements are stacked one on top of another to create particularly sapid wines. The concept of sapidity deserves more conversation that it receives in this ever-warming climate; where acidity may be lacking, sapidity is a reminder that other options remain available to the winemaker seeking vibrancy.

Tannins create the drying sensation felt in various textures and locations in the mouth, as described in the entries on red grape varieties.

Whole cluster fermentation in red wines (the inclusion of whole bunches of grapes in fermentation vessels, not just berries; also known as the use of **stems**) can be perceived on the palate, where it increases pH, giving a softer texture and a very slight oiliness. But perhaps more easily, it is perceived on the nose as a lifted, herbal spiciness – a touch green but with some exotic notes too. In order for whole cluster fermentation to be successful, the stems of the bunches must be ripe, so whole cluster usage may be reduced in cooler or wetter vintages.

For the wine faults of **reduction** and **volatile acidity**, please refer to Wine Faults in Miscellaneous Advice.

Tasting for Grape Variety

Introduction

In the entries that follow, I discuss the characteristics of wines made from each grape variety through the lens of structure. I supplement structure with discussion of a variety's construction, other attributes such as texture, body weight and even (whisper it!) flavour. Each entry concludes with a brief discussion of other varieties with which this variety could be confused, as well as producer recommendations. The next few pages explain these elements in more detail.

I start with white grape varieties, and with the five grapes that are grown throughout the world and made in numerous styles: Chardonnay, Riesling, Chenin Blanc, Pinot Gris and Sauvignon Blanc. I then move on to white varieties more associated with certain regions. I take the same approach with red wines, where the big five are Cabernet Sauvignon, Merlot, Syrah, Pinot Noir and Grenache, before addressing other varieties.

Structure

In the section on white grape varieties, I begin each entry by stating the shape, type and level of acidity inherent to the variety. In the section on red grape varieties, I first state the location, type and level of tannins. Because some of my ideas are abstract and difficult to grasp immediately, I encourage you to read the notes as well as looking at the three summary statements at the top of each entry. Nonetheless, for your convenience I have summarised all the different shapes, locations, types and levels of acidity and tannin in a table in Appendix II (this table is also available for download at vintagevariation.com/beyond-flavour).

One note on structure: having spent a lot of time thinking about structure in major grape varieties, I increasingly notice that *the most celebrated varieties also show the most pronounced structures.* For instance, the big five white and red varieties listed above all have well-defined structures, with the arguable exception of Grenache.

When tasting the big five varieties in each colour, I find it relatively straightforward to identify and describe their structures. But when trying to describe structures of less frequently seen varieties, I find it much harder; partly due to my lack of familiarity with them, but I submit for consideration the notion that we do not see these varieties as often in part precisely *because* they don't have a very pronounced structure. A finely wrought structure is foundational to a great variety.

For tips on tasting blends, see Miscellaneous Advice.

Construction

After summarising the three structural points at the beginning of each entry, I then dedicate one sentence to the 'construction' of the variety. This is my attempt to summarise the 'internal logic' of a variety: how it works as a wine.

In my view, some wines show all the elements of the wine 'pulling together' in the same direction. One example would be Sauvignon Blanc, where the vibrant acidity and the aromatic focus create an ebullient, exuberant, vivacious style. Or Pinot Noir, where aromas, acidity and tannins all seem to aspire 'upwards,' giving lift and a sense of ethereality.

Other wines, however, are more of a 'tug of war' between different elements, all in tension with one another. These elements pull in different directions, and the tension they create is what generates the overall taste sensation of the wine. Often, but not always, this takes the form of elements of the wine balancing one another. Fruit and acidity, for instance. But it can also involve sweet and savoury; the phenolic content in certain whites; or tannins in reds.

Chardonnay, for example, is a variety that combines quite supple, sometimes even soft or generous fruit, with a firm line of acidity. If the acidity were not so firm and consistent, the fruit might collapse in on itself. But the acidity provides the drive and tension that ensures the wine retains its shape. Or in the case of Nebbiolo, delicate, ethereal fruit sit on top of a powerful tannin structure. It is these elements and their interplay that most define varietal style.

Of course, when varieties can be vinified sweet or dry, still or sparkling, trying to summarise a variety's construction in one sentence may be a fool's errand. But my point with the construction idea is to try and establish a common denominator in wines made from the same variety, irrespective of origin or wine style. So inevitably there will be many divergences. But I hope you find the construction sentence a useful shorthand way of thinking about how a variety works in the glass.

Notes

The bulk of each entry is a discussion of the main features of a variety. This includes further explanation of the structure summarised at the beginning of each entry, and the construction. But it also covers aspects such as flavour, texture, colour: anything that can help with understanding the variety.

Please note that I do not cover the rudiments of each variety or where it is grown. If you do not know that Pinot Noir is a light to medium bodied variety, depending on climate, this book is probably not yet for you. My focus is on the granular details of varieties and regions, particularly with reference to structure.

I do not attempt to discuss all varieties. The purpose of this book is to help students understand varieties that they are most likely to encounter in their studies: those most widely found on international markets; so I have stuck to mainstream varieties. Likewise with regions of origin: I am aware that Jim Barry is growing Assyrtiko in Australia (and very nice it is, too), but for the purposes of improving your tasting, it is more sensible to focus on that variety's classic region of origin (Santorini).

Illustration

Each variety entry includes an 'illustration.' I use the term advisedly, because the purpose is to 'illustrate' my description of the variety's structure. It is decidedly *not* a scientific 'diagram,' even in the red wine sections where I indicate where in the mouth you feel the tannins. Instead, the illustrations are simply ways of creatively imagining what I am describing in the text. If you find them helpful, great; if not, please skip over them.

In general, though, the white grape variety illustrations are focused on the *shape* of the acidity, and the red grape ones on the location of the tannins in the mouth, and the type, or texture, of the tannins.

You will find a lot of repetition within the illustrations. That is because, for instance, there are many wines with linear acid structures or tannins felt on the gums. I made the choice to tolerate repetition of images rather than ask the reader to turn back to a previous entry each time to view the appropriate illustration.

Confusions

Of particular use, I hope, will be the 'confusions' section of each variety entry. In my terminology, a 'confusion' is *another grape variety that could be mistaken for the one currently being discussed.* Pinot Noir and Gamay could be confused in a blind tasting, for example. In this section I discuss what I consider to be the most likely confusions for each variety. It cannot be exhaustive: the list would never end. I focus instead on those varieties most likely to be mistaken for the variety in question.

Producers

For each grape variety, I suggest producers whose wines I believe represent classic examples of their styles and should therefore be good examples of their grape varieties. In addition, the wines should be at least somewhat available on international markets (enough volume is produced and distribution is broad) and the wines should be *relatively* affordable. That is, almost all suggested producers' wines are available for under USD $/€60 (in the case of expensive wines like Burgundy or Bordeaux), but much more commonly for under $/€30.

Of course, I could simply list the most famous producers in each region. But with rapidly escalating prices, a list of trophy producers is more likely to be aspirational than practical for wine students. Classic, available and affordable are instead my criteria for the recommended producers.

These producer suggestions are not, and are not intended to be, exhaustive! Please do not be offended if I have not included your favourite producer. There are simply too many to list for many regions, so do not consider my selections as proscriptive: supplement them with your own.

Regional expressions

The discussions of how a variety expresses itself in specific, important regions follow the variety description, so that you can consider both. Both variety and regional details are necessary to formulate a thorough appraisal of any wine. I offer more detailed analysis of wine styles from a handful of classic European regions. In these origins (Bordeaux, Burgundy, Rhône, Piedmont and Tuscany), regional identity is conveyed so strongly that it is possible to pin down characteristics of sub-regions, including villages or even single vineyards. The same is possible in numerous other regions not included here, but I have elected to discuss in detail only those areas where sub-regional specifics are likely to be tested in a blind tasting. I intend no offence to omitted regions.

Enough prologue. On with the main event!

White Grape Varieties

Chardonnay

Shape of acidity: linear, horizontal

Type of acidity: firm, broad

Level of acidity: moderate

Construction: supple fruit shaped by firm acidity

Notes: Chardonnay is the best white grape variety to start with in a discussion of acid structure in white wine. Why? Because Chardonnay has a particularly recognisable and straightforward structure. It is an object lesson in how to understand the concept.

Chardonnay has a powerful, linear acid structure. The acidity is felt consistently throughout the journey of the wine on the palate. This means that the acidity is felt immediately on entry, and remains at the same level throughout, all the way through to the finish. The effect is to create a sense of purpose or direction in the wine; as the acidity courses along, the wine really feels as if it is going somewhere. This sense of direction makes Chardonnay the white wine equivalent of Cabernet Sauvignon.

To expand a little further on this idea, I think of Chardonnay as having a *horizontal* acid structure, because of the consistent perception of the acidity — there are no peaks and troughs of intensity — and because of its 'straight as an arrow' sense of direction.

This horizontal quality in turn relates to how the acidity interacts with the wine's body. In some wines (see Sauvignon Blanc), the acidity can remain quite separate from the fruit. Not so with Chardonnay. In Chardonnay, the acidity is completely integrated into the body of the wine. There is no gap between the fruit and the acid; the acidity is enveloped by the fruit, and in turn, the acidity is the motor which propels the fruit through to the finish. Because of this integration, the acidity is generally felt where the fruit is felt: on the tongue.

A word on the *type* of acidity: because it is so linear and consistently felt, I always consider Chardonnay to show firm, broad acidity. Broad in the sense of 'broad shouldered' — giving shape to the wine. I use the analogy of a rail in a closet on which the clothes hangers hang. The acidity is the horizontal rail, and the hangers are the other components of the wine: the fruit, the body, the oak etc. All 'hang' on to the acidity to find their correct place in the wine; it is the acidity that gives shape to the whole.

The level of acidity in Chardonnay varies greatly between growing regions and wine styles, but is most commonly at a moderate level.

Visually, I conceptualise the body of Chardonnay as a cylinder, and within it is the consistent, horizontal line of acidity.

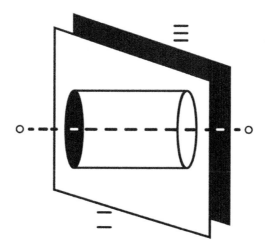

In terms of construction, Chardonnay tends to show quite supple, generous or soft fruit which provides a contrast to the focused, directional acidity. This contrast between acid structure and fruit is the 'x factor' of the variety and central to understanding how Chardonnay works in the mouth.

Confusions: Chardonnay has many potential confusions, but by looking for the linear acid structure you can eliminate some (Chenin Blanc, Riesling, Marsanne). Pinot Gris and Semillon have a similar linearity, but the acidity has more energy and vibrancy. Many Italian white varieties also exhibit a linear shape; please see each entry for distinguishing features, but look out for the trademark Italian, pithy, slightly bitter, phenolic content, less common in Chardonnay.

Producers: see below under each region of origin.

Chardonnay by region

Champagne: see Sparkling Wine.

White Burgundy

White Burgundy is Chardonnay *par excellence* and manages to achieve a degree of terroir expression in a few villages that is unrivalled in the world.

Whether in Chablis or in the Côte d'Or, premier and grand cru wines are the most ripe, concentrated, intense, complex examples of their origins.

Chablis

Chablis shows Chardonnay's linear acid structure to full effect. In flavour terms, it shows a chalky minerality and a marked salinity. The fruit is almost an after-thought. I often find a satiny, pearl-like texture to the wines, which is not so strange given that oyster shell is such a common descriptor of the aromas. Look out for honeyed notes with age. **Producers:** JPB Droin, Bernard Defaix, JC Bessin, William Fèvre, Christian Moreau, EE Vocoret, La Chablisienne.

Corton-Charlemagne

This famous grand cru appellation gives a particularly expansive wine of real grand cru dimension. Given the large size of the cru, there are many different expressions available. But in general, look out for a powerful structure, a rich texture and concentrated fruit with popcorn and opulent orchard fruits as common flavours. Corton-Charlemagne shows true grand cru body and ripeness but possibly lacks the tension and complexity of the Montrachet grands crus. **Producers:** Bonneau du Martray, Bouchard Père et Fils, Louis Jadot, Joseph Drouhin.

Meursault

Traditionally, Meursault is the land of hazelnuts and dairy richness. These days, that style is out of fashion. You are much more likely to find the Coche-Dury style: reductive (see Wine Faults), tight, tense and nervy, an easy confusion with Puligny-Montrachet. The difference? Meursault's nuttiness means that the fruit is not as pure as in Puligny (or as prominent as in Chassagne). Consider Puligny if you think Meursault, and vice versa. **Producers:** Bernard-Bonin, Benjamin Leroux, Bouchard Père et Fils, Olivier Leflaive.

Puligny-Montrachet

Puligny is the quintessence of fine white Burgundy: linear, taut, pure and particularly mineral (resinous). Puligny wines have a particularly noticeable and powerful Chardonnay linear structure. They are often made in a somewhat reductive manner. **Producers**: Alain Chavy, Jean Chartron, Olivier Leflaive, Henri Boillot, Jacques Carillon.

Chassagne-Montrachet

As befits the most southerly of the three great villages of white Burgundy, these are the richest, most opulently-fruited wines of the region. The best examples are stacked with ripe citrus and orchard fruits, and, in body, are particularly round and generous while retaining firm acidity, tension and chalky minerality. **Producers:** JN Gagnard, Paul Pillot, Michel Niellon, Joseph Colin.

St. Aubin and the Côte Chalonnaise

St. Aubin is a good value source of classic white Burgundy: tense, concentrated and mineral, perhaps just lacking some of the flair of the more famous villages. The Côte Chalonnaise, just south of the Côte de Beaune, is home to Rully, a good source of ripe but dry Chardonnay in a traditional Burgundy style, albeit at a slightly humbler quality level than the Côte d'Or. **Producers:** Hubert Lamy, F & D Clair (St. Aubin); Dureuil-Janthial, Jaeger-Defaix (Rully).

Maconnais

These are generally soft, giving wines appropriate for their more southern origin. The best examples, though, still show some chalky minerality, tension and moderate (c. 13.5%) alcohol. Pouilly-Fuissé is the sub-region of the Maconnais which achieves the greatest quality, and premiers crus have been permitted since the 2020 vintage. Macon produces very good Burgundy, but rarely achieves the precision of the Côte de Beaune: it is riper and rounder. **Producers:** Verget, Héretiers du Comte Lafon, J. Desjourneys, Guffens-Heynen.

USA

Within California, a range of styles is available, making it difficult to generalise about them. There is plenty of the rich, oaky, buttery style, especially at the lower end of the price scale. What these wines share with more ambitious Californian styles is fruit concentration: there is never any shortage of that. Examples from Napa can easily top 14.5% alcohol.

There are also many producers making restrained wines in cooler sites in Santa Barbara and the Sonoma Coast, including some who play with reduction (see Wine Faults). All of the above also applies to Oregon, where more restrained, Burgundian styles are being made, albeit with considerable fruit ripeness compared to French examples.

Whatever the US origin, in American Chardonnay, look out for fruit ripeness, fruit purity and the fingerprints of the winemaker on the wine (lees, bâtonnage, oak, reduction). **Producers:** Sandhi, Au Bon Climat (Santa Barbara); Ramey, Hanzell, Lioco (Sonoma); Groth (Napa Valley); Chalone (Monterey); Walter Scott (Willamette Valley, Oregon).

Australia

Margaret River Chardonnay tends to be a little richer than styles from further east in Victoria, South Australia or Tasmania. This seems to be a winemaking choice rather than being due to climate. Nonetheless, Margaret River can combine the virtues of tension, ripe but not overwhelming fruit and dry minerality.

Winemakers in Adelaide Hills, Yarra Valley, Tasmania and elsewhere in the south-eastern part of the country are making less classic new world styles of Chardonnay. Here, more chiselled, 'slimline' styles are popular, some of which even imitate Chablis. But the fruit remains considerably riper and a bit softer than Chablis; that is, the acidity showcases the slightly cooler style, but the fruit remains resolutely non-European in its warmth. **Producers:** Shaw and Smith (Adelaide Hills); Giant Steps (Yarra Valley); Vasse Felix (Margaret River); Tolpuddle (Tasmania).

New Zealand

Chardonnay could be New Zealand's best variety, but, in the headlong rush to sate the world's demand for Sauvignon Blanc, the country has somewhat neglected it. The climate here is quite Burgundian and so is the style: limpid, pure, with a stony minerality and sometimes a touch of reduction. It is very easy to confuse New Zealand Chardonnay with Burgundy, not least because both use French oak; the giveaway is the slight additional fruit ripeness and purity of New Zealand. **Producers:** Kumeu River (Kumeu); Dog Point (Marlborough); Neudorf (Nelson).

For all other countries producing Chardonnay, please refer to the country overview guides in Tasting for Region of Origin, and simply apply to Chardonnay.

Riesling

Shape of acidity: vertical

Type of acidity: steely

Level of acidity: high

Construction: acidity is the backbone around which all the other elements of the wine circle

Notes: Riesling is another variety with a prominent acid structure. In fact, acidity is the defining feature and organising principle of Riesling; however sweet or dry or floral or petrol-scented the wine is, acidity is the first thing to think about and to comment on.

Riesling almost always has high levels of acidity. That is the easiest aspect of Riesling to understand. Riesling is a cool climate variety which flourishes in sites that allow it to ripen slowly, gradually increasing aromatic and flavour complexity. The kinds of sites that allow for this are also ones that preserve acidity very well.

Like Chardonnay, Riesling has a very specific shape to its acid structure. Interestingly, it is almost exactly the opposite of Chardonnay. Where Chardonnay has a horizontal acid structure, Riesling has a vertical acid structure. What does that mean?

In Riesling, the acidity feels like a vertical bar or pole right through the body of the wine. The other elements of the wine – the fruit, the sugar etc – all circle around it, but the acidity stays firm, immovable and upright. In Riesling, the acidity is the backbone of the wine.

Where Chardonnay has a direction and linearity to it that gives a sense of movement, Riesling, by contrast, tends to feel more static on the palate. It is not in such a rush as Chardonnay to get somewhere, because the vertical acidity seems to 'pin down' the wine in one spot, like a stake.

Another way I think of this vertical acidity is like a fireman's pole, not just because it is vertical, but because of the quality of Riesling acidity. Riesling has a steely acidity; it seems to glint in the light, like steel. Numerous other analogies spring to mind, however: Riesling's acidity is like a ship's anchor, the anchor and chain holding the wine in place; or it is like a maypole, with the dancers being the other elements of the wine, circling around the acidity. To see a rather impressive visualisation along these lines, search on YouTube for Mexico's *Danza de los Voladores*, in which, once again, the central pole is analogous to Riesling's unmoving, vertical acidity.

Whatever the growing region, Riesling shows high levels of steely acidity, with a 'vertical' structure. The notes below should help define region of origin a little more closely.

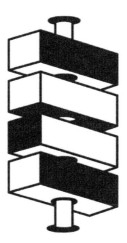

Confusions: Riesling is usually quite distinctive thanks to its brilliant acidity and luminous fruit. In Alsace, other varieties may show a similar texture, but look out for the vertical acidity (also likely to be at a higher level than other varieties). Austrian Riesling is fruitier than the more savoury Austrian Grüner Veltliner. In sweeter styles, Riesling lacks the funkiness of Loire Chenin Blanc and is very rarely as sweet as Sauternes, Tokaji or other botrytis wines.

Producers: see below under each region of origin.

Riesling by origin

Germany

The growing regions of Germany are all quite different, with strong terroir expressions in each. Add to this both Trocken (dry) and sweeter (Prädikat) styles, and the picture quickly becomes complex. But here are some general pointers for identifying regions of origin.

Mosel: in sweeter styles, very light and delicate, with an incredible poise and nervy tension between sugar and acidity: Mosel really walks the tightrope as it maintains the balance between the two. These are particularly precise, pure, ethereal wines. Trocken wines (which in the Mosel are becoming increasingly common) are light (12% alcohol) and precise; they lack the powerful structure of Trocken wines from warmer regions such as Rheingau or Pfalz. **Producers:** Willi Schäfer, Dr. Loosen, Carl Löwen, Selbach-Oster, Clemens Busch, JJ Prüm, Heinrichshof, Weiser-Künstler.

Saar and Ruwer: now officially designated as Mosel, these smaller tributary regions nonetheless have their own identities. Both are even cooler than the Mosel proper. Prädikat wines can be absolutely featherweight and yet packed with intensity of flavour (particularly in the Saar). Trocken wines tend to retain their full permitted allowance of 9g/l of sugar (including at Grosses Gewächs level) to offset their high acidity. **Producers:** Karthäuserhof, Maximin von Schubert (Ruwer); Zilliken, Peter Lauer (Saar).

Nahe: among German Riesling regions, the Nahe is often forgotten by tasters in favour of the better-known Mosel or Rheingau. This is unfortunate, because the wines are equally outstanding. The Nahe is more similar stylistically to Mosel than any other region, but it does not quite have the knife-edge balance or tension of Mosel. It is just a touch rounder and fuller in body. **Producers:** Dönnhoff, Gut Hermannsberg, Diel, Schäfer-Fröhlich, Krüger-Rumpf.

Rheingau: the Rheingau produces Riesling that is more powerful than either the Mosel or the Nahe. Trocken styles can be oily in texture, with stone fruit or even tropical fruit ripeness. Prädikat styles are firmer, broader, less nervy and more concentrated than in either the Nahe or the Mosel. It seems the future for Rheingau will lie in dry wines. **Producers:** Robert Weil, Leitz,

Breuer, Spreitzer, Künstler (a slightly different, richer style from the town of Hocheim).

Rheinhessen: some Prädikat wines are still produced here, but the best wines from these warm sites are Trocken. These are powerful wines, stacked full of spice and minerality, and can be intensely dry (especially from the red slate soils above the Rhine near Nierstein). They have a cleaner, less oily texture than the similarly concentrated wines from the Rheingau. Rheinhessen wines show an ambition comparable to the greatest dry whites anywhere. **Producers:** Wittmann, Gunderloch, Keller, St. Antony.

Pfalz: Pfalz is much warmer than sites further north, so expect fewer Prädikat styles and greater amounts of full bodied, Trocken styles. Some even see new oak. The Pfalz Riesling style is a world away from the tension and poise of the Mosel and lacks the earthiness of Rheinhessen. Instead, the wines can be exuberantly fruity and concentrated – more like Austria's Wachau or France's Alsace regions than other parts of Germany. But Pfalz shows more typically German precision and purity of fruit than those regions do. **Producers:** Bassermann-Jordan, von Winning, Bürklin-Wolf.

Outside Germany

Alsace: if there is one word to describe Alsace Riesling, it is *phenolic*. These wines have an abundance of grip and texture on the palate which can even assume the form of creaminess. Alsace Riesling tends to be full bodied, concentrated, often with rather elevated alcohol (14%+ alcohol is not uncommon for grands crus) and, at higher levels, can be a touch off-dry with an oily texture. Alsace Riesling can be quite a baroque wine in the sense of being particularly generous and intense in many aspects: body, fruit, alcohol and texture.

And the wines *can be* – but not always – among the most petrol-scented of all Rieslings. They also have a whiff of slate and/or smokiness, as so many wines from volcanic soils do. They often have a deep colour – presumably due to the skin contact that also gives them the phenolics. The most obvious confusion here would be with Austrian styles, especially those from the Wachau. But the Austrian wines show more precision, energy and more zesty (or tangy) acidity than Alsace.

Producers: Hugel, Trimbach, Weinbach, Émile Beyer, Boxler.

Austria: Austrian Rieslings more resemble Grüner Veltliner than they do many other styles of Riesling. The acidity is tangy (just like Grüner's) as opposed to steely. Kamptal (especially) and Kremstal can offer pure, crisp, mineral expressions, while the Wachau tends to be more baroque, rich and oily, or even creamy.

Wherever they are from, Austrian Rieslings are always dry, medium- to full-bodied, concentrated wines with some phenolic grip, making Alsace an understandable confusion. But Austrian Riesling is far more energetic than the softer Alsace profile, with bright fruit and tangy acidity. Austrian Riesling may be distinguished from Grüner Veltliner by its different acid structure (consistently present rather than Grüner's peaks and troughs), and its emphasis on fruit rather than on Grüner's more savoury, earthy flavour profile.

Producers: Alzinger, Nikolaihof (Wachau); Hirsch, Loimer (Kamptal); Nigl (Kremstal).

Australia

Look out for low pH in Australian Riesling. Low pH (which is different from high acidity, although Australian Riesling certainly does have high acidity) gives a hard mouthfeel which can resemble phenolic grip (but note most Australian Riesling does not undergo skin contact). The petrol note is common across all regions even in a wine's youth. The standard is for the wines to be fully dry, unless a deliberate choice has been made otherwise. (This is in contrast to New Zealand, where most Riesling has some residual sugar). Australian Riesling generally should not be confused with European examples, because of the typically non-European emphasis on purity of fruit expression. Clarity and primacy of fruit are always pointers towards a non-European origin; this is certainly true with Riesling.

Clare Valley: the classic source of Australian Riesling. Clare gives intense lime flavours, a powerful, steely, vertical acid structure, and is always very brisk and clean. Chalky, detailed and intense, and occasionally so dry that the wines are austere. **Producers:** Grosset, Mount Horrocks, Jim Barry.

Eden Valley: a bit softer, with slightly higher pH and lower acidity than Clare. Eden shows more floral and berry notes and is less limey and edgy than

Clare. Some wines can have a jasmine scent and more minerality than Clare. **Producers:** Pewsey Vale, Penfolds Bin 51.

Western Australia: these are riper, softer and more fleshy and generous than Clare/Eden with more weight and dimension of flavour, including stone fruit. Western Australian Riesling lacks the intensity of Clare and can show less mid-palate concentration and structure. **Producers:** Frankland Estate (Frankland River); Leeuwin (Margaret River).

USA

Washington State in off-dry mode is a Mosel style, but with greater breadth and fruit generosity and not as much elegance. It can be quite appley. Finger Lakes Riesling offers high acidity and aromatic expression but can lack mid-palate concentration. **Producers:** Ste Michelle (Washington); Hermann J. Wiemer, Dr. Konstantin Frank (Finger Lakes).

Chenin Blanc

Shape of acidity: crescendo

Type of acidity: bracing

Level of acidity: high

Construction: powerful acidity cuts through fruit and sugar

Notes: Chenin Blanc is one of the more misunderstood white varieties. It is misunderstood largely because tasters often consider it a relatively difficult variety to identify. But *au contraire*, I believe that if you understand its acid structure, it should be one of the easiest to spot, precisely because it has such an unusual and distinctive acid structure.

Chenin has particularly high acidity. Wherever it grows, the acidity does not seem to change. It is always high. And more to the point, it has a particularly bracing quality — many Chenin wines reveal themselves when, after five seconds or so on the palate, you have to spit or swallow because it is almost painful not to. The acidity is so high that it is almost uncomfortable: you find yourself bracing when you experience it!

But it is the shape of the acidity that really sets Chenin apart. Chenin Blanc has a crescendo-shaped acid structure. On entry, the wine feels quite soft and a bit structureless (especially in examples with residual sugar). But as the wine remains on the palate, the perception of the acidity increases and increases and increases...until the taster must spit or swallow. Like a crescendo in music, Chenin's acidity seems to amplify the longer the wine stays in your mouth.

Compare to Chardonnay or Riesling, where the acidity is felt immediately when the wine hits the palate and stays constant throughout: this is a totally different experience. Here, the acidity comes on gradually but then dominates the finish.

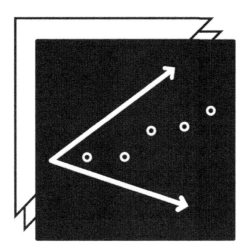

As an aside, Chenin Blanc justifies its place in the top five great international varieties list not because it is grown in so many places worldwide but because of its outstanding stylistic adaptability, its complexity and its longevity. Stylistically, it is available as still or sparkling, as bone dry or very sweet; the best examples from the Loire can show complexity comparable to any white wine on earth and can age for 50 years or more, especially the sweet examples. It fulfils all the criteria for a so-called 'noble' variety.

Confusions: Chenin's crescendo acidity distinguishes it from almost all other white varieties, especially Chardonnay, which is probably the most likely confusion when coming from South Africa. In France, cooler-climate whites such as Chablis might generate confusion, but in addition to the different acid structure, the funky, unusual flavour profile of Chenin should separate it from Chardonnay. Grüner Veltliner also exhibits a rising acidity on the finish, but the tangy, 'reverberant' quality of that acidity is very different to Chenin. Albariño is more phenolic.

Producers: see below under each region of origin.

Chenin Blanc by region

France, Loire

Vouvray: the most classic rendition of the grape comes from Vouvray. Completely dry wines are a little unusual in Vouvray; even *sec* styles may contain up to 13g/l of sugar. Vouvray tends to show a powerful acid structure to make a broad-shouldered wine. Vouvray may be Chenin Blanc's most distinctive expression in flavour terms – almost pungent with bruised apple and saline notes, along with a rasping, chalky minerality on the finish.

Sweeter styles can be made with and without botrytis influence. High acidity balances the sweetness, and the sugar seems to bring out the funky, salty, baked apple aromas all the more. **Producers:** Huet, Vincent Carême, Aubuisières.

Montlouis: in terms of sweetness, Montlouis is often a drier wine than Vouvray, and many Montlouis wines are fermented to full dryness. These are often a touch lighter in body than wines from Vouvray, but the best show a lingering chalky minerality and great acid structure. **Producers:** Taille Aux Loups, Jacky Blot, François Chidaine.

Savennières: Savennières is one of the most distinctive but rarely tasted white wines in the world. Fully dry, Savennières is usually fuller bodied and higher in alcohol than Vouvray (it can reach 14%). It can be very austere – almost joyless! – in its dryness. However, age is the cure, and with a few years' bottle age, Savennières starts to adopt flavours similar to oak influence (although it is usually fermented and aged in stainless steel) and shows a toasty note. The latter point confuses tasters who think it could be Hunter Valley Semillon, but the difference in body weight (heavier), alcohol (higher) and acid structure (crescendo rather than linear) should eliminate confusion. **Producers:** Baumard, Pierre Bise.

There are other Chenin Blanc wines from the Loire, including from Saumur, which tend to be fully dry, taut, but not quite so powerful as the Savennières style. And a final note on Loire Chenin flavour profile: a 'cidery,' oxidative note is a feature, not a flaw, of many Loire styles; the naturally appley flavours of the variety occasionally take on that more funky dimension even without the wines being made in a natural, minimal sulphur regime. The cidery note should not be considered the fault of oxidation.

South Africa

South African Chenin has a richness and roundness reminiscent of new world Chardonnay. It is enough to make you imagine that the wine had undergone malolactic fermentation. But no; like Loire Chenin, South African Chenin does not typically undergo malolactic. So although the wine is soft and rich on entry, the crucial clue is the finish, where the piercing acidity reveals itself, just like in Loire versions.

South Africa Chenin shows an abundant, tropical fruitiness – especially guava – that could not be more different from the savoury, salty earthiness of the Loire. **Producers:** Badenhorst (Swartland); Raats, Mulderbosch (Stellenbosch).

Pinot Gris

Shape of acidity: linear, horizontal

Type of acidity: tingly, zesty, humming

Level of acidity: moderate

Construction: a lively line of acidity provides a counterpoint to the soft fruit

Notes: Pinot Gris/Grigio may not seem like an obvious variety to include as one of the five important white grape varieties. But it has all the attributes necessary: stylistic diversity, including dry, off-dry and sweet styles; the capacity for complexity and ageworthiness and a range of growing regions in Europe and beyond.

Pinot Gris does not have as prominent an acid structure as the varieties previously discussed, making it a little more tricky to identify – especially in the sometimes neutral Grigio style. But nonetheless, it is possible to make a few generalisations.

First, Pinot Gris usually shows medium levels of acidity, though occasionally it is high (e.g. in Alto Adige). It is a mistake to think that Alsatian Pinot Gris has low acidity; usually it is moderate and firm, but sometimes it can be soft (which may be the cause of the misconception).

Second, Pinot Gris shows a linear acidity, similar to that of Chardonnay. The acid is perceived as a straight line through the heart of the wine, steady and regular from the beginning to the end. The difference between Chardonnay and Pinot Gris is that Pinot Gris's acidity has a slightly more tangy or 'electric' quality to it. Where Chardonnay's acidity is firm and undemonstrative, Pinot Gris's is zesty and alive. It almost hums with life, like when you stand below high-tension electricity pylons — you can hear the wires humming with energy.

Note that Semillon, like Chardonnay and Pinot Gris, has a linear acid structure. But Semillon is identifiable for showing particularly electric acidity, much more so than Pinot Gris. So for varieties with a linear acidity, the 'electric' quality of the acidity increases from Chardonnay to Pinot Gris and peaks with Semillon.

Finally, whatever the style of the wine, Pinot Gris shows acidity that is well integrated into the body of the wine, as with Chardonnay. The acidity is 'tucked into' the body, so as to be quite unobtrusive. The exception are wines from Alto Adige, whose acidity is particularly electric and seems to stick out slightly from the body of the wine.

Confusions: Chardonnay may be the most obvious confusion for its supple fruit and linear acidity, but look for additional texture in Pinot Gris when made in the Alsatian style and more lightness of touch than almost all Chardonnay when in Pinot Grigio form. Pinot Gris has more fruit than Pinot Blanc from Alsace.

Producers: see below under each region of origin.

Pinot Gris by region

Alsace: textural richness is a hallmark of Alsace wines in general, and particularly for Pinot Gris. In everyday wines, this expresses itself as a softness and a generosity of fruit. Higher end examples, including grand cru wines, show a viscous, even oily texture. These wines tend to have some residual sugar, and higher alcohols — 14% or more.

At all quality levels, Alsatian Pinot Gris tends to show some bitterness on the finish, which helps give the wine bite and freshness. Some examples can be particularly textured with a phenolic content that dries out the gums and cheeks.

Occasionally, you find deeply-coloured examples thanks to the pink hue of the grape. Pinot Gris is not an especially aromatic variety, but the best Alsatian examples display ginger and spice and a typical Alsatian smokiness. **Producers:** Hugel, Trimbach, Weinbach.

Northern Italy/Friuli: the Pinot Grigio style here yields wines of limited concentration, complexity and ageworthiness, with some exceptions, usually those which include phenolic content for structure and freshness. But, in general, these are light-bodied, pale-coloured wines with moderate acidity that may feel anywhere from soft to firm. The finish is honeyed. Alto Adige examples may be the most interesting in Italy: here, the acidity is high and focused and gives a vibrancy and life to the wine that Friuli examples can lack. These wines can also be interestingly floral. **Producers:** Jermann, Venica and Venica (Friuli-Venezia Giulia); Terlano, Elena Walch, Abbazia di Novacella, St. Michael-Eppan (Alto Adige).

Oregon: the Oregon style is the Alsatian style. These are full bodied, rich, powerful whites with considerable fruit concentration, but may be distinguished from Alsace by being more purely fruity compared to the earthy, smoky, sometimes funky Alsatian examples. **Producers:** Eyrie Vineyards, Bethel Heights.

New Zealand: these wines tend to show at least some residual sugar, a lifted aromatic profile and sometimes quite a deep colour. This is the Alsatian style, but in slightly cooler climate mode, giving a lighter body, more fruit purity and precision, although the alcohol can still be high (up to 14%). **Producers:** Greywacke, The Ned, Loveblock (Marlborough); Mt. Difficulty (Central Otago).

Sauvignon Blanc

Shape of acidity: spherical

Type of acidity: prickly, unintegrated

Level of acidity: high

Construction: acidity around the edge of the mouth and exuberant aromatics create an outward-facing wine

Sauvignon Blanc is a very distinctive variety, and most tasters will recognise it without too much confusion. But while you might intuitively know what it is by the pronounced aromas alone, there are still plenty of other aspects of the wine to discuss.

Fortunately, Sauvignon Blanc has a pronounced acid structure. Sauvignon Blanc always has high levels of acidity, like Riesling. What is most interesting about its acidity is its type: it is spiky or prickly. Where a variety like Chardonnay has acidity with no hard edges, Sauvignon Blanc is completely the opposite: here the acidity has a distinctly prickly, spiky sensation and a 'spherical' shape.

What does it mean to say that Sauvignon's acidity is 'spherical'? If you imagine holding a small ball in your mouth, the edges of the ball, touching the edge of your mouth – cheeks, gums, roof and floor of the mouth – is where you physically feel the prickly acidity. 'Round' or 'circular' could describe it as well, but 'spherical' captures the three-dimensional quality of the acidity around all the edges of your mouth. Often you notice Sauvignon's acidity on the tongue to start with, but it always finishes around the edge of the mouth.

A couple of points emerge from this spherical shape to help the taster. First, shape is very helpful in the few examples of Sauvignon Blanc that do not show prickly acidity. Top quality Sancerre and Pouilly-Fumé with limited yields tend to smooth out the rough edges of this rather aggressive acidity and make the wine more mellow. But the acidity is still spherical and found around the edges of the mouth.

Second, Sauvignon Blanc acidity is perceived distinctly and separately from the body of the wine. That is, the acidity is felt in one part of the mouth (around the edges) while the fruit is felt elsewhere (in the middle of the mouth, on the tongue). This lack of integration of the acidity stands in contrast to Chardonnay and Pinot Grigio, and even Riesling. But once again, this detachment of acidity and fruit only seems to be a function of everyday examples of the variety; when made with high quality fruit, the whole becomes more harmonious and integrated.

In terms of construction, Sauvignon Blanc is an 'outward looking' wine. That is, the acidity seems to aspire outwards to, and even beyond, the edges of the mouth. This sensation is emphasised further by Sauvignon's famous aromas, which want to escape the bounds of the glass: they soar upwards. A variety like Chardonnay has a calm, composed integrity, at ease with itself; Sauvignon always seems to aspire beyond itself.

The spherical acidity of Sauvignon situates the variety's structure around the edges of the mouth. And this, in a very different mode, is exactly what we find in the red Bordeaux varieties – to at least some of which Sauvignon Blanc is a genetic relation. That is, the tannins in the two Cabernets and Merlot are felt on the gums. In the case of Cabernet Sauvignon, its famously light mid palate (see further below under Cabernet Sauvignon) is underscored by the considerable tannic heft felt on the gums. Likewise, the high levels of acidity of Sauvignon Blanc felt all around the edges of the mouth can highlight the lightness of fruit in the middle. Even across colours, there is some continuity of construction between the Bordeaux varieties.

Confusions: less aromatic varietal Sauvignon Blanc could be confused for similarly prickly, spiky wines with detached acidity, like Muscadet or Aligoté, but Sauvignon has more fruit than both. Sauvignon Blanc-Semillon blends could be confused with richer wines like Chardonnay, but Sauvignon's high acidity should be the distinguishing feature.

Producers: see below under each region of origin.

Sauvignon Blanc by region

Loire: it is becoming increasingly difficult to generalise about the Loire style, now that many producers seek increasing ripeness and aromatic expression, *à la* New Zealand. But in general, one still should look for drier, more savoury styles from France. Likewise, the textbook differences between Sancerre and Pouilly-Fumé, the two premium Loire appellations for the variety, never hold in reality as well as you hope they will.

In general, though, I find Sancerre a more floral, perfumed, aromatic expression, with many of the best examples being quite chalky; Pouilly-Fumé can be more flinty (I prefer that to 'smoky') and more green-fruited (gooseberry) as opposed to floral. Lesser regions of the Loire show strong varietal characteristics (i.e. herbaceous aromas, spiky acidity) but tend to be less concentrated and complex. **Producers:** André Dezat, Gérard Boulay, Henri Bourgeois, Alphonse Mellot.

Bordeaux: it is unfortunate how often tasters forget about this huge production region for Sauvignon Blanc. Most AC Bordeaux Blanc will be made from a majority of Sauvignon Blanc, which ripens easily and with high yields here. These simple wines scarcely show more body than those from further north in the Loire, especially if they are vinified in stainless steel.

More ambitious versions will be blended with Semillon, to achieve a medium-bodied wine often with some oak influence. Generally speaking, in all these everyday wines there is less varietal expression than in the Loire. The Sauvignon Blanc here is not quite as pure as in the Loire, and it can become a little 'sweaty' smelling. In general, though, unblended versions should be crisp and aromatic.

Blended white Bordeaux has an enviable virtue: it seems to achieve complexity quite easily. These are aromatic wines with ample, zesty, fresh fruit but with a noticeably dry, savoury finish – a winning combination. The Semillon offers texture and fruit in the middle of the palate, while the Sauvignon acidity is felt around the edge.

Higher-end dry versions, especially from Graves and Pessac-Léognan, are likely to include some Semillon and at least some new oak. Semillon adds texture and body. In premium examples, Semillon also brings the creamy textural richness and smoky, lanolin notes that make these wines such good candidates for ageing in French oak. The Semillon counteracts the additional richness by supplementing the acidity with a jolt of electricity: these are very bright, lively wines in spite of their weight (see further under Semillon). **Producers:** Marjosse, Bauduc, Grand Village (Entre-Deux-Mers/Bordeaux); Clos Floridène, Carbonnieux, Couhins-Lurton, Petit Haut Lafitte (Graves/Pessac-Léognan).

For **Sauternes**, see Sweet Wines.

New Zealand: this is the light bodied, high-acid Loire style but with even more perfume. The aromas here lean towards the tropical and away from gooseberry. There are good oaked versions which offer some additional smoky depth. **Producers:** Greywacke, Dog Point, Seresin, Villa Maria (Marlborough).

Chile: the most notable feature of Chilean Sauvignon Blanc is that the naturally herbaceous character of the variety is exaggerated by the 'green,' pyrazine style that is typical of so many Chilean wines. In other words, you are putting 'green on green,' so these wines can be very pungently herbaceous indeed. In terms of fruit profile, they show more restraint and fewer tropical notes than New Zealand. **Producers:** Errázuriz, Leyda, de Martino, Arboleda, Concha y Toro.

USA: while there are many unoaked versions from the US, the most well-known style is Fumé Blanc. This should be easy enough to identify by the smoky oak notes, but because of the generally warmer climate from which the wines come, the acidity can be subdued and the aromas not very herbaceous. These wines can lean more towards stone fruits in flavour and show more mid-palate texture and richness. This is a good opportunity to look for the spherical acidity as the key to the variety. **Producers:** Robert Mondavi Fumé Blanc, Groth, Spottswoode, Massican (Napa Valley).

Melon de Bourgogne (Muscadet)

Shape of acidity: supernova

Type of acidity: jagged, sharp

Level of acidity: high

Construction: lees and fruit in the middle of the palate balance acidity around the edge

Notes: Structurally, Melon de Bourgogne's closest analogue is Sauvignon Blanc, with which it shares high levels of sharp, spiky, jagged, tart acidity that is often disconnected from the body of the wine. But there is more of a dynamism to the acidity of Melon than that of Sauvignon. In Muscadet, the acidity seems to 'explode' outwards. It is perceived at first on the tongue but then expands outwards to the edge of the mouth. This is what I call the 'supernova' effect, and it is a distinctive attribute of this variety.

Melon also diverges from Sauvignon aromatically — Muscadet is a neutral variety, and also in its winemaking, where it is commonly matured on its lees. Muscadet's ageing *sur lie* adds a creamy texture felt on the mid palate and a bit of additional body weight, balancing the high acidity. Without this additional richness, Muscadet would be an even lighter wine than it already is. Muscadet has a dry, salty finish.

Confusions: less aromatic examples of Sauvignon Blanc share some features of Melon de Bourgogne discussed above, but in addition to the marginally different acid structure, Sauvignon simply has more fruit. Chablis shows a linear acid structure, and Aligoté is more powerfully structured. Albariño has more fruit.

Producers: Pepière, l'Ecu, Sauvion, Luneau-Papin, Cormerais, Morandière (Muscadet).

Aligoté

Shape of acidity: spherical

Type of acidity: sharp, jagged

Level of acidity: high

Construction: supple fruit shot through with powerful, jagged acidity

Notes: Once obscure, Aligoté is an increasingly fashionable variety, thanks in part to climate change, which enables the variety to ripen more readily than previously. It may be confused with Muscadet or even less expressive styles of Chablis given that, like Melon de Bourgogne and some cool climate Chardonnay, Aligoté, too, is a rather neutral, high-acid variety. But the type of acidity is quite different from the others.

Aligoté has a rasping, searing, rapier-like acidity which is particularly potent and incisive. This jagged, sharp acidity is the real standout feature of the wine, in a way that could not be said even of spiky Sauvignon Blanc. But Aligoté resembles Sauvignon Blanc in another way: the acidity is felt around the edge of the mouth, giving a spherical shape.

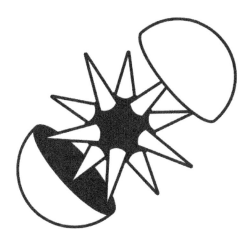

Look also for a crunchy, phenolic grip to the wine; there can be real substance and structure to Aligoté, buttressed by the powerful acidity. An unexpected blackcurrant flavour note can appear in Aligoté, and on the finish, there can be a saline, occasionally smoky or mineral note.

In terms of construction, like its fellow Burgundian variety Chardonnay (there is some genetic relationship between the two varieties), Aligoté shows quite a soft or supple fruit character, offset by the acidity and phenolic grip.

Confusions: other, less fruity, high-acid wines could be confusions: Muscadet is lighter all round; Chablis more linear; Pinot Blanc richer in texture.

Producers: de Villaine (Bouzeron); Sylvain Pataille, Benjamin Leroux, Lafarge (Bourgogne Aligoté).

Gewürtztraminer

Shape of acidity: ball, point

Type of acidity: soft

Level of acidity: low

Construction: phenolic grip structures the rich, oily fruit and compensates for low acidity

Notes: Gewürztraminer is an aromatic variety first and foremost, and most tasters will be familiar with the rose water, spice and Turkish Delight notes that make it so distinctive. But there is a lot to say about other elements of the wine, too.

Gewürztraminer is a full-bodied variety with high alcohol (14%+) and considerable textural richness. The viscous, bath oil, almost 'slippery' texture is quite distinctive. Although other Alsatian wines also show an oily texture, perhaps because of Gewürztraminer's low, soft acidity, it feels more pronounced here. The acidity does not have a pronounced shape; instead it is more like a point or ball on the tongue, gently radiating outwards through the fruit.

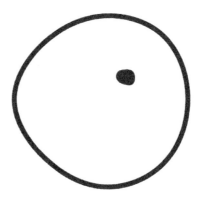

Most Alsace Gewürztraminer is never fermented completely to dryness: 10-20g/l of residual sugar is common. Late-harvest and botrytis versions will display higher levels of residual sugar, greater intensity and complexity of flavour, and additional warm spice notes.

In all Gewürztraminer, look out for the characteristic pithy phenolic bitterness on the finish. The skin contact which gives rise to the phenolics is necessary because the flavour of Gewürztraminer is in the skins. The phenolics not only offer a savoury component to the wine in the place of the understated acidity, but also provide structure (like tannins in red wines) and some dry bite or attack to a wine than would otherwise be a little sweet tasting, shapeless and soft.

Confusions: Among aromatic varieties, Gewürztraminer is less grapey, aromatically, than Muscat or Torrontés. Viognier has a plush texture with oily hints, but not at the same level as Gewürztraminer's oiliness.

Producers: Hugel, Trimbach, Weinbach, Zind-Humbrecht (Alsace).

Muscat

Shape of acidity: linear

Type of acidity: firm

Level of acidity: moderate

Construction: aromatically focused with enough acidity to keep the fruit bright

Notes: Muscat is not, in fact, a single variety, but a family of varieties sharing a common name. Muscat Blanc à Petits Grains, common in the south of France, offers the most distinguished, complex aromatic profile. Muscat of Alexandria is grown around the Mediterranean basin and is generally confined to sweet wine production. Muscat Otttonel is the Alsatian Muscat; it lacks the aromatic intensity of the other two, although it does ripen well in this more moderate climate.

The two Mediterranean Muscats in dry form offer the trademark bright, grapey aromas, a light to medium body and moderate levels of firm, linear, bright acidity. (See the section on fortified wines for Vins Doux Naturels).

In Alsace, Muscat Ottonel shows some textural oiliness similar to Gewürztraminer, but the body is lighter and the acidity firmer, fresher and brighter. Muscat's grapey, floral aromatics can be a touch one-dimensional compared to Gewürztraminer. Alsatian Muscat is more often vinified fully dry than Gewürztraminer.

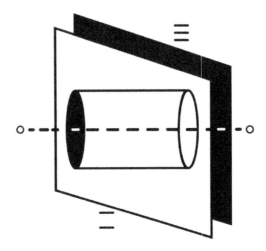

Confusions: Muscat is more grapey, aromatically, than Viognier or Gewürtztraminer, and shows less richness of texture. Torrontés is the most logical confusion, thanks to its similar aromas, but it shows more acidity than Muscat and usually less purity of grapey aromas.

Producers: Trimbach, Weinbach, Sparr (Alsace); Tetramythos (Peloponnese, Greece); de Martino (Itata, Chile).

Pinot Blanc

Shape of acidity: linear

Type of acidity: bright

Level of acidity: moderate

Construction: rich fruit and texture cut by bright acidity

Notes: One of the common misconceptions about this variety is that it is totally bland with no redeeming features. In the right hands, Pinot Blanc can be a wine full of interest. It shows a rich, soft texture, in common with the other Alsace varieties. But the acidity here is higher than you first think – usually at least medium and firm and certainly higher than Gewürtztraminer or Pinot Gris. The acidity is linear. In Alsace, Pinot Blanc is usually a dry, somewhat neutral, musky, simple everyday wine in still form (it can give, often blended with Auxerrois, a pleasant, chalky crémant).

Pinot Blanc is not an aromatic variety, but in the many excellent German examples (confusingly named Weissburgunder), it does achieve considerable breadth of fruit flavours not usually found in Alsatian versions. In German examples can be found a rich array of stone and even some tropical fruit flavours, with layers of texture. Examples from northern Italy, meanwhile, can be very zesty and fresh.

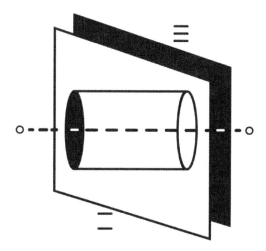

Confusions: from Germany, Weissburgunder is rich enough to be confused for Chardonnay, but if anything, shows more ripeness and exotic fruit than Chardonnay. In Alsace, Pinot Blanc lacks the fruitiness and spice of Pinot Gris and the acidity of Riesling. In Alto Adige, expect a greater ranger of fruit, spice and mineral aromas and flavours than Pinot Grigio normally shows.

Producers: Hugel, Trimbach, Weinbach (Alsace); Wittmann, Gunderloch, Krüger-Rumpf (Germany); Terlano, St. Michael-Eppan (Alto Adige, Italy).

Marsanne

Shape of acidity: circle

Type of acidity: bright

Level of acidity: moderate

Construction: soft, ripe fruit and rich texture overlays subtle acidity and dry minerality

Notes: Marsanne makes a rich but dry, full-bodied wine with a moderate level of bright acidity which seems to circle the tongue. The best examples (from Hermitage) have some resemblance to the Montrachet grands crus in their weight and complexity but are a little more earthy and honeyed with a viscous texture. At the core of the wine is a dry, flinty minerality. Cloudy apple juice is an idiosyncratic but apposite aroma note for Marsanne, while its finish shows a slightly oxidative, bruised apple note.

Rhône Marsanne is usually blended with at least a proportion of Roussanne, which contributes acidity and is more aromatic than Marsanne. Roussanne means 'russet,' and sometimes (but not always) contributes a golden colour. Roussanne has moderate levels of firm acidity and a clean (as opposed to viscous) texture. Its most characterful attribute may be its herbal tea aroma.

Early harvested dry Australian Marsanne (from producers such as Tahbilk) is similar aromatically to Australian Riesling or Hunter Valley Semillon (toasty and limey), but lacks the really crisp acidity of either, and, at only 11% alcohol, shows lower alcohol than dry Riesling would.

Confusions: Roussanne has more acidity and a cleaner texture than the thicker Marsanne. Marsanne is richer and riper than Burgundian Chardonnay, while still remaining resolutely in the European, dry, savoury white wine world. It is less fruity than white southern Rhône blends such as those from Châteauneuf-du-Pape.

Producers: Clape (St. Péray); Graillot, Jaboulet Mule Blanche (Crozes-Hermitage); JL Chave (Hermitage).

Viognier

Shape of acidity: linear

Type of acidity: steely, bright

Level of acidity: moderate

Construction: textural plushness balanced by phenolic grip and steely acidity

In the most famous region of Viognier's Northern Rhône home, Condrieu, Viognier is full-bodied and intense, with a slightly oily, viscous texture and some phenolic grip, probably deriving from the variety's thick skins. The phenolics give a pithy bite, helpful given that the acidity is only of a moderate level, albeit with a steely brightness and linearity to it.

Alcohol often reaches 14% or higher, contributing to the sense of weight on the palate. One of the peculiarities of the style is that although this is a concentrated, full, rich wine, it is somehow not fruit focused. There is ample fruit present, but the texture, body and alcohol seem to be the focal point rather than the fruit.

The famous floral perfume – also easily noticeable when blended even in small amounts into Côte Rôtie – may, however, be masked by use of new French oak, which is common in Condrieu and contributes some creaminess to the texture and a sense of sweetness to the fruit. It may also offer some structure to this most richly textured wine.

It is important to note that some examples of Condrieu simply are not particularly aromatic. And even if they are, the reputed orange blossom note that all wine students are taught to look for, may not be present. Instead, the earthy savouriness typical of so many French wines emerges (which is naturally a far less lifted perfume than floral aromas). A smoky, musky note is common.

Either way, the soft, plush texture of Condrieu may be considered a more reliable and consistent characteristic than the aromas. It may not be a coincidence that Viognier shows a textural plushness similar to the variety with which it is sometimes co-fermented: Syrah.

Elsewhere in the world, Viognier may not show such body weight, textural finesse and dramatic aromatics, but the muskiness and oily texture remain consistent.

Confusions: among other aromatic varieties, Viognier is less grapey than Muscat or Torrontés, and shows less of the peculiar spicy aromatics and bitter finish of Gewürztraminer.

Producers: Georges Vernay, Guigal (Condrieu); Yalumba (South Australia).

Other white wines from the Rhône Valley: further south in the Rhône, Grenache Blanc tends to be the predominant variety in Châteauneuf-du-Pape Blanc. Grenache Blanc offers generous fruit and body, with a soft texture and limited acidity (sound anything like its red version?). It is most conspicuous by its tendency to show an oxidative, appley aroma, even in youth. In Châteauneuf blends, the acidity comes from Bourboulenc and Clairette. None of these varieties has an abundance of fruit flavours, but the wines at their best are pleasantly citrusy, with moderate acidity, a full body and a gentle lemony perfume on the finish.

Semillon

Shape of acidity: linear, horizontal

Type of acidity: electric, buzzing, zesty

Level of acidity: high

Construction: fruit plays a secondary role to brilliant acidity and a tactile texture

Notes: Varietal Semillon is virtually never seen outside Australia, where it is a speciality. Worldwide (including in Australia), it is blended with Sauvignon Blanc. Wherever it comes from, its acidity has a similar shape to Chardonnay; that is, it is constant, linear, and really races through the wine. But Semillon's acidity is more zesty or buzzing with energy (or 'electric' – see Pinot Gris), while Chardonnay's is more firm. Semillon acidity is usually high.

Semillon shows a little phenolic, tactile mid-palate texture, which contributes body and balances the vibrancy of the acidity. In monovarietal examples, Semillon is not an overtly fruity variety; instead relying on the acidity and texture to supply interest and complexity. Blending with Sauvignon Blanc gives fruit; botrytis in sweet versions adds flavour dimension.

Confusions: for Chardonnay, see the discussion above. Early picked Marsanne from Australia can be a confusion with Hunter Valley Semillon, but Semillon has more acidity and overall vibrancy. Australian Riesling has more fruit and alcohol than Semillon. Savennières can have a similar toasty flavour profile, but Savennières' alcohol is considerably higher (13.5-14%), its body considerably weightier and of course it shows the trademark Chenin 'crescendo' acidity.

France: For Bordeaux blends and producers, see Sauvignon Blanc.

Australia: In Australia — and particularly in the Hunter Valley, where the mono-varietal style reaches its acme — Semillon is an early-picked, low alcohol (11%), high-acid style, unoaked, steely and quite neutral in its youth. However, it develops beautifully in bottle to show lime marmalade and toast notes.

In Margaret River, Sauvignon Blanc-Semillon blends are common. Usually these are light bodied, with high acidity and aromatically reveal Sauvignon Blanc by their herbaceousness. How do you know they are not 100% Sauvignon Blanc? Because of the slightly oily texture which Semillon contributes.

Producers: Tyrrell's, Brokenwood, Mount Pleasant (Hunter Valley); Voyager Estate, Vasse Felix (Margaret River).

Grüner Veltliner

Shape of acidity: rollercoaster

Type of acidity: tangy, humming, buzzing

Level of acidity: high

Construction: rich texture balanced by tangy acidity and savoury flavour profile

Notes: When you know what to look for, Grüner Veltliner stops being the understated, even neutral variety that many tasters imagine, and instead becomes one of the more characterful European white varieties.

The best way of identifying it is, as usual, by its acid structure. Grüner's acid structure I compare to a rollercoaster, or, for the mathematicians among you, to a sine curve. That is: the acidity is rather low when the wine first hits the palate, then climbs quickly. Just as quickly, it falls off again, only to return, stronger than ever, on the finish. Up, down, up again.

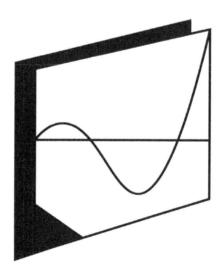

The quality of Grüner's acidity is always tangy. That is, the acidity seems to reverberate in the mouth, or positively hum or buzz with life. (Although note that Riesling from Austria also seems to have a tangy quality, so this may be related more to origin than variety). Beyond the acid structure, Grüner has other important distinguishing features. Most noticeable is its savoury flavour profile, which tends not to show ripe, juicy fruit, instead focusing on peppery, spicy, earthy notes.

Grüner is a wine of great texture. Especially in higher quality examples, at first sip Grüner can resemble Chardonnay, with its generous, soft texture. But then the tangy acidity kicks in, and the experience is quite different. This disjunction between soft texture and tangy acidity is further exaggerated in those examples with a creamy or oily quality; these soft textures contrast particularly vividly with the acidity. The well-known white pepper flavour note of the variety adds a textural quality in the context of the tangy acidity; both create a sense of vibrato, or reverberation, in the mouth. And a final note on construction: Grüner can be quite phenolic; contributing to the dry, savoury quality of the wine, and contrasting with any textural richness or softness.

At lower quality levels, Grüner is light bodied, crisp and savoury with a touch of white pepper, lime, agave, peanuts and watercress. Among the three premium regions – Kamptal, Kremstal and Wachau – there are distinctions. Kamptal and Kremstal tend to make clean, crisp, mineral styles, often fermented in stainless steel. Of the two, Kamptal tends to be a bit more precise and driven while Kremstal is a bit softer.

But Wachau, with its quality levels, is quite different. In order to get the ripeness necessary for the higher levels such as Smaragd, some botrytis is often present. The result is wines of much greater richness and body than the other regions, often aged in oak, and showing creaminess on the palate and a flamboyant, baroque complexity.

Confusions: Albariño is the most common confusion. Grüner's acid structure is slightly different: you feel the acidity continually, albeit at different levels in Grüner, whereas in Albariño, the acidity retreats entirely in the middle. Grüner is also more mineral and earthy while Albariño is more saline, and while Grüner does show some phenolic grip, Albariño shows more. Chenin similarly shows rising acidity on the finish, but lacks the tanginess of Grüner.

Producers: Loimer, Bründlmayer, Hirsch (Kamptal); Salomon Undhof, Moser, Stadt Krems, Nigl (Kremstal); Alzinger, Nikolaihof (Wachau).

Albariño

Shape of acidity: wall to wall

Type of acidity: zesty, tart

Level of acidity: high

Construction: phenolics and acid structure take the lead over fruit

Notes: Albariño follows Grüner Veltliner here because the two are so often confused by tasters. But, in fact if you begin with acid structure, the two show divergences immediately. Albariño (Alvarinho in Portugal) has a 'wall-to-wall' acid structure. Upon entry, the acid hits the palate like a wall, but quickly retreats almost entirely. But on the finish, the wall of acidity returns. This differs from Grüner Veltliner in that Grüner's acidity is always more incrementally felt than suddenly appearing.

The perception of this wall-to-wall acid structure in Albariño is enhanced by the high levels of phenolic grip that is so characteristic of the variety. Like Assyrtiko, it is a variety that shows phenolic grip consistently. It is discernible by the slightly bitter, pithy, chewy hardness in the wine around the edge of the mouth and on the finish. When paired with its powerful acid structure, the phenolics make Albariño one of the most structured of all white grapes.

The combination of phenolics, acidity and the variety's trademark saltiness all contribute to the wine's fresh, sapid style. Some examples even contain some dissolved carbon dioxide, which further enhances the freshness.

The combination of a distinctive acid structure and the presence of powerful phenolics in the wine make Albariño easily identifiable without reference to flavours. Indeed, Albariño is only semi-aromatic, and, rather than being fruit-focused, is a variety more led by structure. Nonetheless, a notable saltiness, an orange blossom aroma and a touch of lime pith from the phenolics may be used as confirmatory evidence. Albariño is usually only a medium-bodied variety but can taste like a full-bodied wine thanks to its potent structure deriving from its thick skins. Probably for the same reason, Albariño can have quite a golden colour in the glass.

N.B.: in the previous edition of this book, I argued that Albariño has a square acid structure, with the 'walls' making the sides of the square, and the acidity retreating to the floor and ceiling of the mouth in between. However, some tasters did not pick up on the floor/ceiling aspect of the description, so now I prefer to focus on the 'wall to wall' description.

Confusions: Grüner Veltliner is covered above. Albariño has more fruit and structure than fellow salty wine Muscadet, and more structure, complexity and depth than Godello or other northern Spanish varieties. It is more overtly fruity than the more savoury Assyrtiko. From Rias Baixas, it is more fruity than in single variety Vinho Verde expressions, where the salinity comes to the fore.

Producers: Granbazán, Pazo de Señorans, Forjas del Salnés, Albamar (Rias Baixas); Valados de Melgaço, Soalheiro (Vinho Verde).

Viura (Macabeo)

Shape of acidity: diffuse

Type of acidity: soft, fruit-wrapped

Level of acidity: moderate

Construction: gentle acidity, oak and umami give complexity to softly textured fruit

Notes: Viura in Rioja (predominantly, but elsewhere in Spain too) is interesting for two reasons. Neither of them is that it is a very characterful variety in terms of fruit profile or structure: it is not. First, it has an outstanding capacity to age. And while rather neutral when made in stainless steel and released early, with oxidative (oak) ageing, it can develop a nutty complexity. Its second virtue is that, in good examples, Viura from Rioja is transparent to its origins in having, at its core, a dark, umami, savoury note. This becomes more visible with age, as the fruit fades. This savoury note is a characteristic of the best red Rioja too, and the capacity of Viura to express it is clearly a mark in the variety's favour.

Moderate levels of soft, diffuse acidity enveloped in the soft, ripe fruit, moderate alcohol and a medium weight body do not do much to distinguish Viura, so look out for any nutty oxidative notes of age, the creamy texture of the fruit and that umami heart.

Confusions: the soft fruit may invite comparisons with Chardonnay, but Chardonnay has more direction and focus, with a more prominent acid structure.

Producers: CVNE, López de Heredia, Muga (Rioja).

Verdejo

Shape of acidity: linear

Type of acidity: zesty

Level of acidity: moderate

Construction: zesty acidity and phenolic grip shape generous fruit and creamy texture

Notes: Verdejo from Rueda is a wine full of energy and personality, with the concentration and structure for mid-term ageing. It is certainly an aromatic variety, but if you are expecting a light, fresh style after the pungent nose, à la Sauvignon Blanc, you will be surprised. Verdejo shows some phenolic structure, and moderate (occasionally high) levels of linear, zesty acidity. The fruit can have a creamy texture. This is a mid-weight white, packed full of flavour (white stone fruits, melon, star fruit and herbal notes), revealing its warm climate origins.

Confusions: the traditional confusion is with Sauvignon Blanc, but, while aromatic, Verdejo is far less herbaceous, has lower acidity and more phenolic content. It is not as structured as Albariño and shows more aroma and fruit than Viura or most Italian whites.

Producers: Marqués de Riscal, José Pariente, Ossian (Rueda).

Vinho Verde varieties

Shape of acidity: rinse, shower

Type of acidity: tart, prickly

Level of acidity: high

Construction: tart acidity and a light body create a fresh, zesty wine

Notes: Vinho Verde is increasingly made in more complex single variety examples (see below), but the commercial bulk remains a blend of indigenous varieties (Alvarinho, Loureiro, Trajadura, Arinto, Avesso). It is distinguishable in spite of its simple, understated citrusy flavours because of two features: its low alcohol (usually around 11%) and the dissolved carbon dioxide that is a hallmark of the style. Spot those, and you cannot be in many other places. More ambitious styles feature more concentrated fruit and body weight.

The acidity in Vinho Verde feels like a shower, or rinse: the little points of acidity are dotted throughout the fruit, in the same way that dissolved carbon dioxide behaves. This 'rinse' effect generates a sense of brightness to the wine, not least because the acidity is tart or prickly: you cannot help but notice it as it 'prickles' your mouth.

The best Vinho Verde, often coming from the warm Monção e Melgaço subregion, is made from single varieties such as Loureiro and especially Alvarinho, which is far less fruity here than over the Spanish border in Rias Baixas. In these wines, a medium body, 13%+ alcohol, high acidity, salty

minerality and concentrated fruit are the hallmarks. These wines have sufficient concentration to improve for up to five years when made by top producers, such as those named below.

Confusions: light, fresh, saline wines like Muscadet or, naturally, Albariño, could be confusions. Lower-end Vinho Verde is lighter and lower alcohol than all of them, with little to no phenolic texture. Single variety Alvarinho is usually not confused with Albariño from Rias Baixas in spite of its geographical proximity; the Vinho Verde version being far more restrained in terms of fruit, emphasising salinity and vibrancy rather than fruit and density.

Producers: Soalheiro, Valados de Melgaço, Adega de Monção, Quinta do Ameal.

Assyrtiko

Shape of acidity: square

Type of acidity: powerful

Level of acidity: high

Construction: powerful acid structure and phenolics dominate

Notes: Assyrtiko is one of the world's most characterful white varieties. On Santorini, it makes an aromatic, medium- to full-bodied wine with a powerful, square acid structure. The acidity is felt on the gums, roof and floor of the mouth; in this formulation, the gums are the sides of the square, and the roof and floor of the mouth the top and bottom.

Exaggerating the square-shaped acidity is the strong phenolic bitterness, also felt on the gums and on the finish. Given the overlap between the two, it can be hard to know where the acidity ends and phenolics begin. Either way, thanks to this powerful structure, Assyrtiko is one of the more obviously ageworthy European white varieties.

Assyrtiko is intensely dry with very little focus on fruit; the focus is instead on the acidity, the powerful herbal, smoky, salty, mineral flavours and the lime zest phenolic bitterness on the finish. The variety's low pH also enhances the 'hard' texture and tartness of the acidity. Assyrtiko is quite deeply coloured.

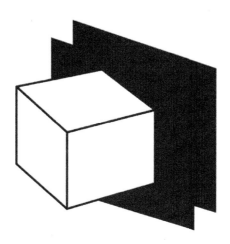

Confusions: Albariño is the most obvious confusion for its similar focus on structure and restrained fruit expression, but even without being a fruit-led wine, Albariño shows more fruit than Assyrtiko. The phenolic structure in Assyrtiko is more powerful, the body fuller and the alcohol often higher; the Greek variety is simply a bigger wine all around.

Producers: Sigalas, Hatzidakis, Argyros, Gaia (Santorini).

Furmint

Shape of acidity: shower, rinse

Type of acidity: prickly, zesty, 'popping'

Level of acidity: high

Construction: intense freshness and a light body leant weight by phenolic texture

Notes: Dry examples of Hungarian Furmint are light to medium bodied, with two defining features: a strong phenolic grip on the gums and a brilliant acidity. The acidity is so bright it feels like a shower of pinpricks of light around the tongue, bursting or popping in the middle of the fruit. The effect is to give the acidity a particularly prickly or zesty quality. In flavour terms, good examples show a pleasing spiciness and smokiness.

For sweet examples, see Sweet Wine.

Confusions: The combination of a rather light body with phenolic grip is an unusual one; lighter examples of Albariño could be confused with Furmint, or even Muscadet, but Furmint has more intense acidity than both. Aligoté usually shows more body and a more piercing acidity.

Producers: Disznókő, Royal Tokaji, Patricius (Tokaj).

Torrontés

Shape of acidity: linear

Type of acidity: firm, juicy

Level of acidity: moderate

Construction: aromatically focused, with bright acidity cutting through the soft fruit

Notes: Argentina's signature aromatic white variety is most obviously confused with its parent variety, Muscat, because of its grapey aromas, moderate body and alcohol, slightly creamy or viscous texture and soft fruit. However, Torrontés wines also show a firm, fruity, (occasionally spiky), linear acidity and a touch of soapiness to the texture. A saline note sometimes appears on the finish.

This is an aromatic, fresh, fruity variety, usually without great complexity or length, although more ambitious examples are certainly being made (see producers below).

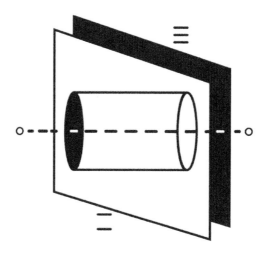

Confusions: due to shared genetic heritage, Muscat is the obvious confusion. Torrontés can lack the purity of grapey flavour of Muscat, and feature a slight rubbery, synthetic note on the nose or finish (see additional comments above).

Producers: Susana Balbo, Zuccardi (Mendoza); Colomé (Salta).

Italian White Varieties

Identifying Italian white varieties — even if you know which country you are in — is one of the hardest tasks in a blind tasting. There is considerable stylistic overlap between varieties, so plenty of consideration should be given for mistakes. One continuity among styles is the generally linear profile of the acid structures. For that reason there is considerable repetition among the illustrations in this section. Linearity is a characteristic of Italian white varieties, and perhaps also contributes to the back palate emphasis in so many of these wines (see Tasting Glossary and Italy in Tasting for Region of Origin): the acidity 'pushes through' to the finish, where the wine really comes alive.

For **Pinot Grigio**, see Pinot Gris.

Garganega

Shape of acidity: linear

Type of acidity: consistent, steady

Level of acidity: moderate

Construction: light and elegant with viscosity, phenolics and minerality for subtle complexity

Notes: Soave's variety cannot be called aromatic, but it usually displays more pronounced aromas than, say, Pinot Grigio. It is a classic Italian, lemony, light-bodied white and displays well-integrated linear acidity. It is distinguishable by its gentle smoky minerality (possibly from its volcanic soils) and a subtle phenolic grip for a little attack and structure. Garganega often shows a very slight oiliness or viscosity. It possesses an understated elegance and complexity that its neighbours often lack, especially on the finish: this is a good example of a back palate wine.

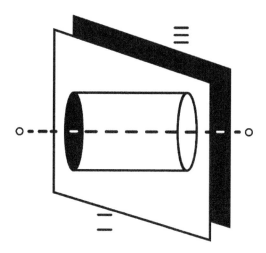

Confusions: many Italian varieties could be confused, especially Pinot Grigio, but the slight smokiness and oily texture are signatures of Garganega from Soave. Verdicchio has a similar body weight but is a bit brisker in texture and nuttier on the finish.

Producers: Pieropan, Inama, Prà, Gini, Danieli, Bertani (Soave).

Cortese

Shape of acidity: linear

Type of acidity: zesty

Level of acidity: moderate

Construction: zesty acidity and slight phenolic bitterness create structure-led wine

Notes: From Gavi, Cortese can be very bland if over-cropped, because it is not an aromatic variety. Better examples show more body (with a touch of creaminess) and a firmer acid structure than Garganega — this is a more substantial wine than Soave. There is also a sense of energy and life from the moderate (sometimes high) zesty acidity, although it is well integrated into the fruit. The finish is very dry and clean. There is a modest expression of citrus fruit and gentle herbal notes, but this is a wine of freshness and structure above all, finishing with the slight Italian phenolic bitterness.

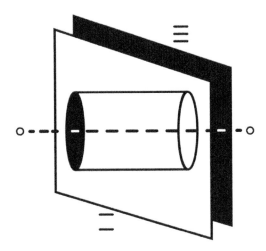

Confusions: Cortese has more fruit than Pinot Grigio and Garganega, but not as much as Arneis. It is more purely fruity than Verdicchio (nuttier).

Producers: La Scolca, Broglia La Meirana, Castellari Bergaglio (Gavi).

Verdicchio

Shape of acidity: linear

Type of acidity: steely

Level of acidity: moderate

Construction: delicate fruit propelled by a steely acidity

Notes: Verdicchio is a fresh, light wine with steely acidity. It can be one of those frustratingly generic Italian white varieties but look out for its pleasant hazelnut retronasal perfume (i.e., it appears after you have swallowed). Verdicchio may be subtle, but the brisk steeliness (or metallic quality) of the acidity propels the wine forward in an enjoyable fashion.

Confusions: Pinot Grigio and Cortese are more fruity and less nutty, and Cortese usually shows more body weight. Verdicchio is cleaner and brisker than Garganega, with its slight smokiness and viscosity.

Producers: Bisci (Verdicchio di Matelica); Bucci, Sartarelli, Andrea Felici, Tavignano (Verdicchio dei Castelli di Jesi).

Arneis

Shape of acidity: linear

Type of acidity: firm

Level of acidity: moderate

Construction: firm acidity and phenolics shape the soft, generous fruit

Notes: Another white variety from northern Italy, Arneis should be more identifiable than neighbours Garganega, Pinot Grigio or Cortese. It is a more aromatic variety, with a candied orange or orange blossom nose. It can offer considerably more body weight and fruit on the palate, some oily texture and good phenolic grip. Because of all the fruit, the acidity can feel lower and softer than in other Italian varieties, but it is still of a moderate level.

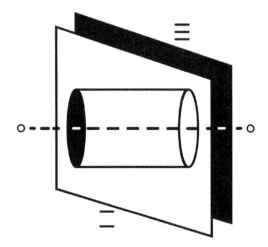

Confusions: If Garganega and Pinot Grigio risk, at times, being a little innocuous, Cortese should be less so and Arneis not at all. That is, Cortese has more fruit and body than Garganega and Pinot Grigio, and Arneis more than all of them. Arneis' aromatics make it more comparable to Vermentino, but Arneis lacks Vermentino's herbal streak and high acidity.

Producers: Ceretto (Langhe); Bruno Giacosa, Vietti (Roero).

Vermentino

Shape of acidity: linear

Type of acidity: firm, zesty

Level of acidity: high

Construction: lively acidity and savoury herbal quality offset the oily texture and rich fruit

Notes: Vermentino is an aromatic variety with some oily viscosity on the palate, high levels of linear, zesty acidity and a strong herbal streak. It has a warm climate's generous fruit, medium to full body, a slight oily texture, and a touch of salinity, adding complexity. Vermentino is appealing because, unlike many Italian whites, its attractions do not require much digging to find: they are immediately and satisfyingly obvious.

Confusions: Vermentino's confusions are likely to be similarly aromatic Mediterranean wines. It is more herbal than Arneis. Southern varieties such as Greco would be a sensible confusion; however, Greco is a bit more phenolic and less overtly fruity than Vermentino. Fiano is less aromatic.

Producers: Antinori, Tesoro (Bolgheri); Argiolas (Sardinia).

Fiano

Shape of acidity: linear

Type of acidity: steely

Level of acidity: high

Construction: a piercing line of acidity cuts through rich, viscous fruit

Notes: In the Fiano d'Avellino DOCG and other regions nearby, Fiano makes rich, viscous, waxy-textured, medium- to full-bodied wines. They rely on their high levels of linear, steely acidity to balance the thick texture. Fiano is not particularly aromatic, showing some stone fruit notes; this is a wine more about texture.

Confusions: Fiano is less aromatic and more acidic than Greco. It has more body and texture than whites from further north in Italy.

Producers: Mastroberadino, I Favati, Ciro Picariello (Fiano di Avellino).

Greco

Shape of acidity: expanding, radiating outwards

Type of acidity: zesty

Level of acidity: moderate

Construction: a full body and an oily texture shaped by phenolic grip and subtle acidity

Notes: Greco is an emphatic wine: aromatic (orange blossom, peach pith, floral, herbal and spicy), full-bodied, with a rich, oily texture and plenty of mouth-coating phenolic grip. The zesty acidity is only of a moderate level and seems to expand outwards from the tongue. Look out for a honied finish along with the usual phenolic bitterness.

Confusions: Greco is more full-bodied, phenolic and aromatic than Fiano. The aromatic style and oily texture makes Vermentino a confusion, but Greco is more phenolic and does not burst out of the glass aromatically in the same way Vermentino does.

Producers: Mastroberadino, I Favati, Benito Ferrara, Feudi di San Gregorio (Greco di Tufo).

Red Grape Varieties

Cabernet Sauvignon

Location of tannin: gums

Type of tannin: grippy, fine grained

Level of tannin: high

Construction: directional tannins and marked acidity produce a streamlined wine with a strong sense of forward momentum

Notes: Cabernet Sauvignon is a good example of a red variety that is easy to identify if you assess the tannin structure but can be quite difficult if you look only at flavours. Cabernet has a powerful and distinctive tannin structure that distinguishes it from other varieties.

Cabernet shows generally high levels of fine-grained, tightly-knit tannins that grip the gums. That is, they are 'grainy' in texture, but the grain is so fine that you hardly notice it. And they are tight rather than loose — their edges are very clearly defined and they do not 'spill out' into the rest of the wine.

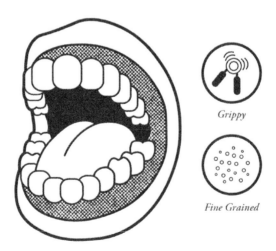

Grippy

Fine Grained

Cabernet tannins are felt on the gums and not on the tongue. This in part explains the oft-repeated assertion that Cabernet has a 'hole in the middle,' because the serious tannic charge renders the focal point of the wine the gums rather than the tongue. A bit like Chardonnay's acid structure among white wines, Cabernet's tannin structure is very linear with a strong sense of direction. That means that the tannins shape the experience of the wine on the palate and, in this case, give the wine a sense of movement or purpose; it is really going somewhere.

Nicolas Glumineau, winemaker at Château Pichon Lalande in Pauillac, remarks that Cabernet tannins are shaped like an arrow. I love this analogy for two reasons. First, what he is referring to is that, like an arrowhead, the tannins taper to a point on the finish. This explains the sense of movement I am describing: the tannins have a point they move towards, on the back palate (the finish). Virginia Willcock, winemaker at Vasse Felix, uses a different analogy to make the same point: Cabernet tannins are shaped like a horseshoe, felt around the gums but coming to a point on the finish.

The second reason I love Nicolas' analogy is that the arrow comparison also reminds one of a road sign, pointing the direction to go in. And that underlines this sense of a journey from the front to the back of the palate that Cabernet's sleek tannins create.

Cabernet tannins, like the tannins of all Bordeaux varieties, are those which seem to taste most like the vine itself. That is, they can be woody, stalky and green if not fully ripe.

Unlike its Bordeaux stablemate, Merlot, Cabernet Sauvignon tends to retain its acidity very well. The acidity gives a sense of energy to the wine, which goes hand in hand with the sense of purpose created by the tannin structure. In other words, its tannin and acidity give a real sense of purpose or drive in

Cabernet, and I think those elements contribute to making Cabernet Sauvignon one of the 'noble' varieties.

Finally, Cabernet is not half so richly fruited as Merlot, and this can also contribute to a sensation of mid-palate lightness, although Cabernet from many non-European origins does not exhibit this lightness.

Confusions: Cabernet can be confused with other Bordeaux varieties, with which it shares grippy tannins felt on the gums. Merlot, however, shows more mid-palate, velvety fruit; Cabernet Franc tends to be less tannic and more aromatic; Malbec has less 'directional' and more sturdy tannins. Carmenère likewise has less polished tannins. Syrah has tannins felt more on the tongue than on the gums, as well as a more seamless fruit texture.

Producers: see under each region of origin below.

Cabernet Sauvignon by region

Bordeaux

Before dealing with the style of the different Cabernet Sauvignon-led appellations in Bordeaux, a few words about the general style of Bordeaux wine. Please read this section in conjunction with the entry on Merlot.

As a wine style different from other Merlot or Cabernet Sauvignon wines around the world, what makes red Bordeaux distinctive? Bordeaux is a wine style built on tannin. Tannin is the *sine qua non* of Bordeaux reds. Other than in a few exceptional vintages, Bordeaux always retains its freshness, but acidity is rarely the most notable characteristic of the wines: tannin is.

Bordeaux is the ultimate dry red wine. When the English use the term 'claret' for red Bordeaux, within that is an understanding that this is a *dry wine*. Even Merlot-dominated wines finish dry and savoury, making Bordeaux a wine style pre-eminently suited to food.

Red Bordeaux is almost always a blended wine. While varietal characteristics are strongly perceptible, in examples above, say, US $25 retail price, place nonetheless predominates over variety. Variety is not the focal point of Bordeaux, and winemakers often get frustrated when asked about the exact composition of their blends, because they believe their terroir speaks more loudly than varieties do.

Red Bordeaux and oak are a perfect marriage. There are a couple of reasons for this. First, the naturally woody, cedary taste of Bordeaux Merlot and Cabernet Sauvignon blend seamlessly with the flavours of new French oak. It is a natural match (as well as supplying the gentle oxygenation these powerful varieties benefit from). Furthermore, the grainy tannins of the Bordeaux varieties seem to match the grain of oak, and the location of both fruit and oak tannins is on the gums (see further on oak tannins in the Tasting Glossary). The longstanding union of oak and Bordeaux reds has a very solid basis.

Merlot dominates Bordeaux in anything other than the cru classé properties of the Left Bank. The perception that Bordeaux is all about Cabernet Sauvignon is simply mistaken. There are only a handful of terroirs in the region that can ripen Cabernet successfully year in, year out. Merlot ripens a lot more easily.

For dry white Bordeaux, please see Sauvignon Blanc, and for sweet white Bordeaux, see Sweet Wines.

Cabernet Sauvignon appellations in Bordeaux

St. Estèphe

Of all the Bordeaux appellations, St. Estèphe is the driest, particularly on the finish, where it can be like licking a dry stone. St. Estèphe tannins are often not well integrated into the fruit (except in very ripe vintages). These are powerful, cassis flavoured wines with huge tannin structures. St. Estèphe performs particularly well in hot vintages, when it can make some of the biggest and most convincing Left Bank wines. St. Estèphe often shows a salty note. **Producers:** de Pez, Tronquoy Lalande, Ormes de Pez, Phélan-Ségur, Lafon-Rochet, Meyney.

Pauillac

Pauillac is the most complete appellation on the Left Bank. The wines show their pedigree initially on the nose, with a complexity and depth that can be beguiling. On the palate, they show considerable concentration and, above all, fruit-wrapped tannins. Here, the tannins are completely integrated into the fruit and are never obtrusive. Even in lesser vintages, the wines finish on fruit. These are intensely ageworthy, powerful wines which show Cabernet Sauvignon reaching its full potential of complexity and beauty. **Producers:** Armailhac, Duhart-Milon, Haut Batailley, Batailley.

St. Julien

St. Julien is the most straight-laced, classic, Cabernet-based wine on the Left Bank. These wines showcase Cabernet's linearity, precision and freshness, with a distinct gravel note to the intense cassis flavours. This is benchmark Cabernet Sauvignon by any standard around the world. Ultimately, St. Julien may lack the thrill of good Pauillac or the aromatic complexity of Margaux, but it is the most reliable, consistent appellation on the Left Bank, in good vintages and bad. **Producers:** Lagrange, Langoa Barton, Beychevelle, Gruaud-Larose.

Margaux

Margaux suffers from inconsistency, and often needs a warm vintage to thrive. Although still Cabernet Sauvignon-led, the wines here have considerably more Merlot than further north in the Médoc, so are less varietally obvious than the northern trio of St. Estèphe, Pauillac and St. Julien. But in a good vintage, Margaux produces the most spectacularly perfumed wines anywhere in Bordeaux. They are only mid-weight and rely on elegance and finesse to succeed. **Producers:** Brane-Cantenac, Giscours, Issan, Rauzan-Ségla.

Pessac-Léognan

Pessac is unusual among cru classé Bordeaux appellations for not having a dominant grape variety. Although Cabernet may be a slight majority in many wines, often the split with Merlot is close to 50-50. That blend is what gives its distinctive qualities: a rich mid palate *à la* Pomerol, but a linearity and directionality typical of Cabernet. If the wine does not scream any particular appellation, it is worth considering Pessac. And Pessac can also be soft and generous – not as opulent as Pomerol of course, but with greater richness on the palate than you might expect from the nose. In flavour terms, it can have a very distinctive warm bricks, chimney ash, cohiba cigar and peat taste. **Producers:** Domaine de Chevalier, Malartic-Lagravière, Haut Bailly.

Cabernet Sauvignon outside Bordeaux

Tuscany: Cabernet here is used heavily in the Super Tuscans, both in Bolgheri and sometimes in the Chianti zone. There are many Left Bank Bordeaux lookalikes among these wines, but in general, in this warmer climate, the wines ripen more easily and consistently each year than in Bordeaux. The result is wines of greater fruit concentration and ripeness. There is a Mediterranean exuberance — occasionally flamboyance — in these wines that Bordeaux rarely displays. Nonetheless, these remain savoury wines with fresh acidity, so are resolutely European rather than from the new world. **Producers:** Bruciato (Guado al Tasso), Serre Nuove (Ornellaia), Guidalberto/Le Difese (Sassicaia San Guido).

Australia, Margaret River: Margaret River is the last bastion for varietal, leafy Cabernet anywhere in the world. Winemakers here are unafraid to make wines with gently herbal notes. And that is not the only cool climate aspect of these wines. Alcohols are only moderate and acidities notably fresh. Tannins are ripe and soft as opposed to powerful, all of which makes for very easy drinking wines. Finally, the wines often show a 'warm bricks' texture and flavour to them. The only reason not to guess a European origin for these wines is because they are clearly fruit-led rather than savoury. **Producers:** Vasse Felix, Leeuwin, Voyager Estate.

Australia, Coonawarra: these are concentrated, powerful, intense wines with a more prominent tannin structure than those from Margaret River. In spite of the concentrated dark fruit on the mid palate, these wines show a classical, tightly-knit tannin structure which keeps any exuberance firmly in check (as opposed to say, Napa, where the fruit richness wins out). A tobacco/herbal note is common. **Producers:** Wynns, Tolmer, Yalumba.

South Africa: usually Cabernet here is blended with the other Bordeaux varieties here to make full bodied, powerful, earthy styles. The concentration of fruit and elevated alcohol are enough to put you in the new world, but the slightly rustic tannins and earthiness confuse the picture. Bearing in mind the rule of thumb about South Africa — one foot in the old world, one in the new world (see Tasting for Region of Origin) — Bordeaux blends are the classic example of the adage. **Producers:** Kanonkop, Meerlust, Glenelly, Boekenhoutskloof, Rust en Vrede.

Argentina: these are dense, inky, powerful wines with occasionally quite rugged tannins. They are savoury in style, but with a ripeness and density of fruit that is typically new world. **Producers:** Catena, Zuccardi, Achaval Ferrer, DiamAndes.

Chile: I mentioned the directionality of Cabernet, and no country expresses this more vibrantly than Chile. Chile's naturally high acid grapes give a real energy to Cabernet Sauvignon so it seems to race across the palate. Medium to full bodied, Chilean Cabernet usually displays herbal/herbaceous aromatics. **Producers:** de Martino, Concha y Toro, Undurraga, Errázuriz.

USA

Napa: Napa Cabernet is one of the world's most emphatic wine styles. While more restrained styles are being made elsewhere in California, Napa's style remains — with very few exceptions — intensely concentrated and opulent, with dense, glossy, sweet fruit flavours and high alcohol. Although there are high levels of tannin, the tannins are particularly supple and fruit-wrapped, so do not appear as prominent as in other regions worldwide. Grapes from the valley floor tend to give seamless, velvety wines, while those from hillside sites yield intense wines with compact, powerful tannins.

Napa Cabernet frequently includes abundant use of new French oak. Look out, too, for glycerol richness, alcohol-derived sweetness (i.e. alcohol tastes sweet, so when it is as high as it is here, it emphasises the already sweet-tasting fruit flavours) and palate-staining black fruit flavours. These are among the world's biggest Cabernet Sauvignon wines. **Producers:** Groth, Spottswoode (Lydenhurst), Corison, Turnbull, Ramey, Trefethen, Matthiasson, Mayacamas.

Sonoma: these are usually more restrained wines than their neighbours in Napa, with cooler sites even giving some green notes. But Sonoma still shows a sweet, dark fruit core, a powerful tannin structure and usually at least 14% alcohol. There is a balance and harmony to these wines even when young. **Producers:** Jordan, Gundlach Bundschu, Laurel Glen.

Santa Cruz: home to some of California's best wines, even if not as well known as the regions north of San Francisco. Cabernet here tends to be a bit drier and fresher than in Napa, albeit still concentrated and powerful. **Producers:** Ridge, Mount Eden.

Washington State: Washington Cabernets are powerful wines, more akin to Napa than Sonoma. The difference is that while both are loaded with intense dark fruits, Washington is drier and more earthy and savoury. The tannins are powerful and not quite as ripe or fruit-wrapped as those in Napa Cabernet wines. **Producers:** Andrew Will, Gramercy, Hedges, L'Ecole 41, Januik.

Merlot

Location of tannin: gums

Type of tannin: grippy, grainy, clayey

Level of tannin: moderate

Construction: rich, velvety fruit framed by structuring tannins

Notes: In structural terms, Merlot has a lot in common with Cabernet Sauvignon. As with other Bordeaux varieties, Merlot's tannins are felt on the gums. The tannins may not be quite so tightly knit and fine as those of Cabernet, but they are grainy, grippy and fruit-wrapped. They can sometimes feel a bit 'sticky' or 'clayey' (like heavy clay) in contrast to Cabernet's sleek tannins.

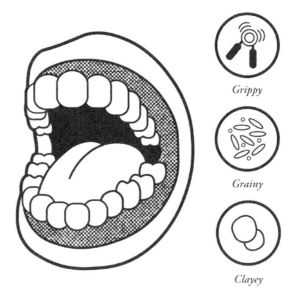

Grippy

Grainy

Clayey

In less ripe Bordeaux vintages, Merlot tannins can occasionally be perceived as woody or stalky, just like Cabernet Sauvignon's. Generally speaking, because of the integration of the tannins into the rich, generous fruit Merlot offers, tannins are less obtrusive in Merlot than they are in Cabernet.

Another difference from Cabernet is that Merlot's tannins are very 'square'. Where Cabernet's are linear and directional, Merlot's tannins are felt so strongly on the gums that they create a 'square' sensation in the mouth: there appears to be tannin on all sides of the mouth. While Cabernet always feels like it is rushing somewhere, this square sensation means that Merlot feels as if it is lingering on the palate: it is more static.

Mid-palate fruit concentration is a key point of difference between Merlot and Cabernet. Where Cabernet's 'horseshoe' tannins can leave a hole in the mid palate, there is no such absence with Merlot, where ripe, succulent fruit dominates.

One interesting aspect of Merlot is that it possesses two textures, experienced simultaneously on the palate. When tasters discuss texture in red wines, there is an assumption that they are referring to fruit texture. But what happens if the tannins have a different texture from the fruit? That is the two-textures situation of Merlot.

The best Merlot wines show a glossy, velvety fruit texture. But Merlot's tannins are grainy and grippy. So on the palate, there is a noticeable difference in the texture of the fruit (velvety) and that of the tannins (grainy). This contrast offers a point of distinction from Cabernet, for example, where the sleek tannins have a similar texture to the elegant fruit.

Merlot can rather quickly lose acidity and for this reason is often acidified (see Tasting Glossary how to taste acidification). At its worst, overripe Merlot is stewy, jammy, shapeless and oxidises easily.

The very lightest Bordeaux styles (e.g. AC Bordeaux from Entre-Deux-Mers) may possess a light body, but most Merlot is medium- to full-bodied.

Confusions: any of the other Bordeaux varieties could be a confusion for Merlot. Cabernet Sauvignon is more linear and directional, has less mid-palate weight and a greater a sense of movement. Cabernet Franc has more acidity, lower tannins and less mid-palate fruit than Merlot (with the exception of warm and hot climates). Malbec has a similar 'square' tannin structure and a static sensation on the palate, but Malbec's tannins are a bit more powerful and rugged, and less well integrated into the fruit. Carmenère similarly has rather unpolished tannins and a distinctive herbaceousness. Syrah can have a similar velvety fruit texture but lacks the square tannin structure.

Producers: see below under each region of origin.

Merlot by region

St. Emilion

St. Emilion classically shows fresh acidity; moderate, firm tannins; bright red fruits and a chalky finish which balances the mid-palate richness supplied by the Merlot. It is a subtle, intellectual, unshowy wine whose virtue rests in its balance, complexity and detail. However, away from the best sites, much St. Emilion can be simply savoury, dry, structured red wine with good concentration but somewhat lacking in excitement. **Producers:** Canon, Moulin St Georges, Fonbel, Corbin, La Serre, Fonroque.

Pomerol

The dominance of Merlot here gives rise to generously fruited, velvety but structured wines whose tannins are always enrobed by fruit. Cabernet Franc can lend some herbal, spicy, tea notes, but in general the Merlot wins out by its velvety — not to say voluptuous — mid-palate texture and rich depth of plummy fruit. In ripe vintages, Merlot risks becoming excessive but in cooler years, can produce remarkably classic wines that appear untouched by the weaknesses of the vintage. **Producers:** Bourgneuf, Gazin, La Grave, Petit Village.

AC Bordeaux (and Pomerol and St. Emilion satellites, Côtes de Bordeaux etc): these are medium bodied wines, red- rather than black-fruited, with a firm line of acidity and moderate, often woody or stalky tannins. Riper vintages showcase some sweetness in the mid-palate fruit, but AC Bordeaux often shows limited fruit. These are quintessentially dry, savoury, earthy French reds. **Producers:** Chenade, Cruzelles, Siaurac (Lalande-de-Pomerol); Clarisse (Puisseguin-St-Emilion); Grand Village, Marjosse, Bonnet (Bordeaux).

Rather few places in the world make good quality varietal Merlot; usually it is part of a Bordeaux blend. Still, a couple of important places make Merlot-led wines outside Bordeaux.

Tuscany: there are a couple of Super Tuscans that include large amounts of Merlot, although the climate is quite warm for the variety. Expect particularly opulent, velvety, hedonistic, sumptuous fruit with seamlessly smooth tannins. The merest hint of a dry finish is all that might put you in Europe rather than the new world. **Producers:** Macchiole, Ornellaia, Masseto.

Hawkes Bay, New Zealand: these wines have a decidedly European style, but they lack the earthiness and savoury quality that typifies Right Bank Bordeaux — New Zealand wines are much more purely fruited. Usually they are quite moderate in alcohol and only medium bodied, as befits the cool climate. They tend to be red-fruited rather than black-fruited. **Producers:** Esk Valley, Craggy Range, Trinity Hill.

California: Merlot is grown throughout the state, but especially in Napa and Sonoma. Here you can expect a plush, rich style, full-bodied and high in alcohol, usually with generous use of new oak in higher quality examples. There are absolutely no hard edges. These are rarely subtle wines! **Producers:** Duckhorn, Stags' Leap, Mayacamas, Frog's Leap, Grgich Hills.

Pinot Noir

Location of tannin: tongue, roof of mouth

Type of tannin: silky, velvety, chalky

Level of tannin: moderate

Construction: acidity, tannins and aromas all rise in the mouth giving a sense of lift and ethereality

Notes: Structure is probably the last thing people think about when it comes to Pinot Noir, but that in itself is a statement about the quality of the variety's tannins. In the simplest examples, it is true that the level of tannins is simply low. Most Pinot Noir, though, has moderate, high quality tannins, which, apart from in very cool vintages in Burgundy, always seem to be ripe. That makes them unobtrusive, and, moreover, the tannins themselves have a juicy, fruity taste, which means they blend effortlessly into the fruit of the wine.

Texturally, Pinot Noir tannins are occasionally chalky, especially in cooler years, but more often they tend to be quite supple, velvety and occasionally silky, meaning that, again, the tannins have a similar quality to the fruit. For all these reasons, tannins are usually quite undemonstrative in Pinot Noir. But do not be fooled: in grand cru Burgundy and other top examples of Pinot Noir, look out for concentrated, compact tannins that in spite of their ripeness can take years to resolve. In terms of location, Pinot Noir tannins initially feel as if they are on the tongue, but then seem to float upwards to the roof of the mouth.

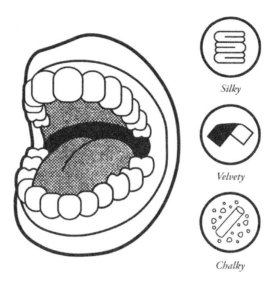

Silky

Velvety

Chalky

This sense of movement in the location of tannins is, I believe, integral to the style of the variety. Because it is not just the tannins that seem to have a certain weightless quality. Pinot Noir can show great perfume within your mouth, while the wine is on the palate, and then retronasally, on the finish. This perfume seems to want to 'ascend,' just like the tannins. Finally, the acidity of Pinot Noir seems to dance around the tongue, giving lift to the fruit. These are the elements that make me think of Pinot Noir as the 'wine of ascent' – everything in it seems to aspire upwards.

Pinot Noir is a particularly aromatic red variety and has a gift for combining its typically sweet-tasting fruit with a savoury or spice note. The interweaving of sweet and savoury, even in young examples, is one of the variety's great virtues. On the other end of the spectrum, lesser examples will simply show an abundance of sweet fruit, which risks being one-dimensional.

In wines where stems/whole cluster are used in fermentation (see Tasting Glossary), expect some additional spice and herbaceous funkiness on the nose, as well as a slightly softer texture overall (because stems increase pH). Whole cluster fermentation makes young wines taste savoury – unexpected and noteworthy here given Pinot's naturally sweet tasting fruit. The effect is most pronounced in new world examples, where the fruit has a sweeter flavour profile than European examples. European Pinot Noir's more savoury fruit profile masks the inclusion of stems to a greater extent, particularly in cooler vintages where the stems may be less ripe.

New oak can work surprisingly well on Pinot Noir, not because (as with the Bordeaux examples) the oak tannins have a similar type and location to the grape tannins, but because the sweet spice, toast and slight smoky flavours of oak can mimic Pinot's flavour profile. Finally, if the wine has undergone pre-fermentation cold maceration (cold soak), expect it to display a deeper, more purple colour.

Confusions: Pinot is certainly one of the easier wines to recognise, but warm climate examples could be confused for a similarly fruity, sweet-tasting style of Grenache. But Pinot Noir is more aromatic and has a more airy quality than the heavier Grenache. Gamay is more chunky and lacks Pinot's silky weightlessness.

Producers: see below under each region of origin.

Pinot Noir by region

Burgundy

Côte de Nuits

When confronted blind with a red Burgundy, my first step is always to try to identify whether the wine is from the Côte de Beaune or the Côte de Nuits, and only later to pin it down to a specific village.

The principal, distinctive characteristics of Côte de Nuits wines for me are an intense spiciness (Vosne or Chambolle) or a shimmering minerality (from Chambolle, Morey St. Denis or Gevrey). I also look for a particularly detailed fruit expression. Dark, brooding complexity is another Côte de Nuits hallmark.

Fixin and Marsannay

These northern villages offer berry aromas similar to Gevrey-Chambertin (although never as delicate and fine) and with sturdier tannins. They lack the overall flair and complexity of Gevrey, although they are attractively fragrant and very authentically Côte de Nuits in their focused, concentrated style.

Producers: Berthaut-Gerbet (Fixin); Pataille, Audoin, Bruno Clair, Mortet (Marsannay).

Gevrey-Chambertin

Gevrey-Chambertin is probably the most misunderstood village in Burgundy, because of the old textbooks that speak exclusively of its 'masculine,' 'powerful' style. It is true that Gevrey has a firm, square tannin structure compared to Vosne or Chambolle. But tannins are scarcely the focal point of the wines. Gevrey is an *intellectual* wine and has two key features: an intricate web of flavours and a particularly well-defined minerality.

Gevrey can be the most *precise* of all the great villages in terms of the clarity of its red fruit flavours – everything is so well delineated, every flavour keenly presented. And then the whole wine is mineral-inflected, a bit like looking across a patch of rock that contains bits of quartzite which glint in the sun – the minerality in Gevrey glints like that. Gevrey perhaps lacks the flamboyance of Chambolle or Vosne, but the complexity and purity more than make up for it. The grands crus rely on finesse and a kind of radiant beauty rather than power. With age, Gevrey becomes particularly gamey and feral. **Producers:** Faiveley, Duroché, Mortet, Fourrier, Jadot.

Morey-St.-Denis

Morey is a small village, and its wines can be earthy and a touch dry and firm compared to the surrounding villages. Grands crus Clos de la Roche and Clos St Denis can be particularly intricate, lifted and elegant, however, combining jewel-like, glossy fruit on the nose with savoury earthiness on the palate. **Producers:** Jouan, Hubert Lignier, Dujac.

Chambolle-Musigny

Chambolle's wines are the most purely *seductive* of any Burgundy village. They have a 'jewel-like' quality, which means the wines possess a kind of sheen overlaying the fruit; a surface which almost shines or glistens, like a diamond in the light. These are particularly velvety wines with a richness that caresses the palate (they possess far more mid-palate richness than Vosne, for example). And, as many wine writers have noted, the Chambolle finish is like a peacock's tail: rather than falling away, the flavours gain breadth and dimension. The aromas can show intense Indian spices (e.g. cumin, cardamom). **Producers:** Felettig, Hudelot-Noëllat, Coquard-Loison-Fleurot.

Vougeot

Village and premier cru Vougeot wines are rare, although they do exist. Grand cru Clos de Vougeot in general lacks the flair of its neighboring villages while nonetheless producing wines of grand cru dimension and weight, with a decided wild, gamey edge. **Producers:** Hudelot-Noëllat, Coquard-Loison-Fleurot, Drouhin.

Vosne-Romanée

Vosne is the most celebrated village for red Burgundy — for good reason. Vosne shows huge aromatic complexity, with abundant Asian spices; a particularly silky texture and a weightless, ethereal quality with a haunting finish. If Chambolle-Musigny is the Pomerol of Burgundy, Vosne is the Margaux. At grand cru level, the additional ripeness of the mid slope expresses itself through greater complexity and beauty, rather than by becoming heavier (with the possible exception of Richebourg, a heavyweight among Vosne's grands crus). **Producers:** Hudelot-Noëllat, Coquard-Loison-Fleurot, Michel Gros, Drouhin, Jean Grivot.

Nuits-St.-Georges

These are earthy, structured wines which almost always lack the grace and spice of Vosne, to which it is so closely located. But their native rusticity and slightly rugged tannins are the charm of these wines, which happily develop their earthy, undergrowth, mulch notes early in life. They can also display a ferrous, iron note early in their development. **Producers:** Robert Chevillon, Henri Gouges, David Duband, Drouhin (for Procès premier cru).

Côte de Beaune

If the essence of the Côte de Nuits is spice or minerality, the Côte de Beaune reds instead show purity of red fruits and floral notes. They can also display a strong iodine, ferrous, iron-y, even metallic quality.

Savigny-lès-Beaune

These are rustic wines which delight with their obvious charms, and uncomplicated, Pinot Noir fruit and feral, gamey notes. **Producers:** Guillemot, Benjamin Leroux.

Corton

Red wines are usually solely from grand cru Corton, a vineyard which probably should be only a premier cru. These are rather structural, dense wines albeit with grand cru dimension. They lack a little excitement. **Producers:** Camille Giroud, Bouchard Père et Fils, Benjamin Leroux.

Beaune

Beaune offers fine, delicate, light red Burgundy with lifted aromatics (particularly of iodine), but lacking by some distance the depth and structure of the Côte de Nuits. Much Beaune vineyard is owned by the town's large négociants. **Producers:** Bouchard Père et Fils, Drouhin, Chanson, Jadot.

Pommard

By Burgundy standards, these are dense, burly, tannic wines which require ageing to open up. A light winemaking touch here is essential, but if you get it, Pommard can be richly red fruited on the nose and palate with a floral perfume on the finish. More and more Pommard wines are being made in this elegant style and as a result show increasing resemblance to their neighbours from Volnay. **Producers:** Comte Armand, Drouhin, Voillot.

Volnay

The most sophisticated red appellation in the Côte de Beaune, Volnay produces pale but fragrant wines with haunting floral aromas. The wines lack the spicy, dark quality of the northern wines and instead rely on a more delicate but nonetheless intricate perfume of red fruits and florals coupled to a silky texture. **Producers:** Comtes Lafon, Drouhin, Clerget, Pierrick Bouley, Voillot.

Côte Chalonnaise

These can be lovely, charming red Burgundy wines from villages like Mercurey (lighter, elegant) and Givry (more concentrated), but, in the final analysis, are wines of fruit rather than the spice or minerality from further north. Nonetheless, they can be very elegant, classic red Burgundy. **Producers:** Faiveley, Lorenzon (Mercurey); Lumpp (Givry); Dureuil-Janthial (Rully).

Sancerre

Sancerre Rouge is a lighter style than village level Burgundy and more akin in weight to Bourgogne Rouge. It can show a distinct chalkiness and pretty aromatics but lacks the complexity of Burgundy. **Producers:** Alphonse Mellot, Pascal Jolivet, Vacheron.

Germany

German Pinot Noir (Spätburgunder) is the best non-Burgundy European Pinot. At its finest, it can offer particularly beautiful aromatics, a velvety texture and long finish. According to Anne Krebiehl's excellent book on German wine, some in Germany refer to Pinot Noir as 'red Riesling.' And that moniker explains the style of the variety from this country.

These are wines of acidity above all, featuring that particularly steely, scintillating acidity that animates German Riesling. Not only does this give great freshness to the wines, it also contributes to the particularly lifted aromatic profile, which features pretty, delicate, red fruit and floral aromas.

On the palate, the fruit can be quite ripe, soft and rich but is given shape by the acidity. The softness of fruit may surprise those who expect German reds to be tart or hard-edged. Tannins are usually of a low to moderate level, as are body and alcohol. These are elementally clean, brisk wines, elegant and well defined, with a lingering perfume – pure Pinot Noir.

Almost half of German Pinot Noir comes from Baden; most of the remainder is split between Ahr, Rheinhessen and Franken. **Producers:** Bernhard Huber, Ziereisen (Baden); Stodden, Meyer-Näkel (Ahr); Keller (Rheinhessen); Fürst (Franken); Rings (Pfalz).

Italy

Pinot Nero from Alto Adige, grown at altitude, is invariably light to *very* light bodied, with a pale colour, delicate aromatics and high acidity. The trademark Italian acidity may be the most obvious clue. Pinot Nero is grown elsewhere in the country, but this is the most noteworthy region of origin. **Producers:** Terlano, Hofstätter, Tiefenbrunner.

New Zealand

These wines are resolutely cool-climate style: light- to medium-bodied, with high acidity, moderate alcohol and clean, crisp (mostly) red fruit flavours with outstanding purity of fruit. New Zealand excels at producing Pinot Noir with great delineation of flavour: every little note is sharply etched. These are fruit-led rather than savoury wines.

Marlborough: the source of a lot of high-volume Pinot Noir; the wines are a bit softer and more generously-fruited than other New Zealand regions. The style is usually easy-drinking: red-fruited and supple. **Martinborough** is a more premium region, making more savoury and more structured, fuller-bodied styles. **Central Otago** offers riper fruit, and its wines show more body, tannin and alcohol than the other regions, often with black rather than red fruit. But the style is still resolutely New Zealand: limpidly pure fruit expression and subtle complexity.

New Zealand producers: Greywacke, Dog Point, Seresin (Marlborough); Craggy Range, Ata Rangi (Martinborough); Felton Road, Two Paddocks, Rippon, Loveblock, Burnt Cottage, Mt. Difficulty (Central Otago).

Australia

Pinot Noir is grown in numerous regions here, making it very hard to generalise. The following regions are the most common: **Tasmania** is the coolest, and the wines from here are closer to the light, crisp, bright New Zealand style than to wines made elsewhere in Australia. **Yarra Valley** makes richer, fully flavoured, more velvety styles, and there is considerable use of whole cluster here, which enhances aromatics. **Adelaide Hills** tends to be a bit cooler in style than Yarra, with more clarity of fruit expression although also expect to see use of whole clusters in fermentation here. **Mornington**

Peninsula retains freshness but can be a little more concentrated and full-bodied than elsewhere in Australia.

Australia producers: Tolpuddle (Tasmania); Giant Steps, Mac Forbes (Yarra Valley); Shaw + Smith, BK Wines (Adelaide Hills); Ten Minutes by Tractor, Moorooduc, Kooyong (Mornington Peninsula).

South Africa

Pinot Noir is not a signature variety for this country, so simply put together varietal and country characteristics for your benchmark: fruit-led wines, but in a more savoury, earthy style than elsewhere in the new world. Examples from Elgin are particularly elegant. **Producers:** Richard Kershaw (Elgin); Bouchard Finlayson (Walker Bay); Storm (Hemel-en-Aarde).

Chile

Chile's high acidity and lifted aromatics express themselves well in Pinot Noir, which here tends to be light- to medium-bodied, pale coloured and delicate, with floral aromas. The perfume is often the principal virtue of these wines. **Producers:** Matetic (Casablanca); Viña Leyda (Leyda); Concha y Toro (Central Valley); Errázuriz (Aconcagua/Casablanca).

USA

Sonoma is a large area, which makes it difficult to generalise, but from here expect soft, velvety, generously-fruited, occasionally opulent, sweet tasting, medium- to full-bodied styles. Often these are more red-fruited than dark, although a sweet cola note is common, as is use of new French oak. These can be quite hedonistic wines. **Producers:** Dehlinger, Kosta Browne, Joseph Swan, Kistler, Lioco.

Sonoma Coast: ambitious examples thus labelled often show considerably lower alcohol (around 13% as opposed to 14%+), high acidity, and at most a medium body, with red rather than black fruit. **Producers:** Failla, Hirsch, Littorai, Peay.

Santa Barbara/Santa Rita Hills: a diversity of styles is available, but in very broad terms, look for more restraint than the rich Sonoma examples, with ripe but measured fruit, reduced oak use and fresh acidity. **Producers:** Au Bon Climat, Sandhi.

Oregon: an increasingly good source of premium Pinot Noir. These tend to be medium- to full-bodied styles, drier than Californian examples, with the best showing considerable intricacy and detail of flavour with a silky texture, making them among America's finest. They can show rather high alcohol for Pinot Noir (14%+). For me, the most obvious Oregon note is the spectacular aromas. I do not know what the cause is, but abundant perfume is an Oregon signature.

Producers: Drouhin, Walter Scott, Cristom, Patricia Green, Bethel Heights, Eyrie.

Syrah

Location of tannin: tongue, gums

Type of tannin: powdery, chalky, velvety

Level of tannin: moderate

Construction: succulent fruit and a seamless texture underpinned by a strong tannin structure

Notes: Syrah can be a trickier wine to identify than most people realise. When it is beautifully aromatic, spicy and full of black pepper, it is easy enough. But when it is not peppery — which is often! — it can be confused with a number of other full-bodied red varieties. Once more, structure is our helpmate.

Syrah is distinctive among full-bodied reds for having moderate to high levels of tannin that are found across the middle of the palate, especially on the tongue. I compare the tannin sensation of Syrah to feeling a knot of tannin on the tongue, tightly coiled, compact and powerful. In some examples of the variety, the tannins seem to be felt all over the palate, unfolding horizontally outwards from the tongue to the gums and cheeks, but the focal point remains the tongue. Once you spot this rather unusual location of the tannins, Syrah becomes consistently identifiable.

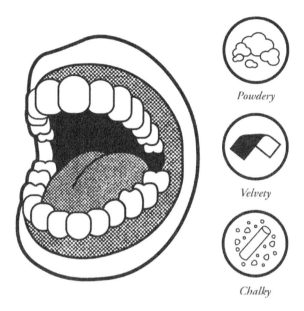

Powdery

Velvety

Chalky

Texturally, Syrah tannins can be a touch chalky or powdery when from European regions of origin. In the new world, however, greater ripeness gives particularly velvety tannins which blend seamlessly into the velvety fruit. In Australia, these smooth tannins are a key distinguishing feature from riper examples of Cabernet Sauvignon, which can also be full-bodied and tannic. But Cabernet always shows more grainy, 'directional' tannin (see Cabernet Sauvignon).

Syrah's fruit is particularly textured: so seamless and velvety that it caresses the palate, even when the tannins are more chalky or powdery, as may be expected in European examples. Along with Pinot Noir, Syrah has the most seductive fruit texture of any red variety.

Good examples of Syrah show that the variety's perfume is not incidental; it is fundamental to the appeal of the wine. Syrah can be intensely aromatic, with deep, heady aromas of dark fruits, spice and earthiness – a perfume you can almost sink into, and which develops with bottle age. It is a deeper perfume than, say, Pinot Noir's (more flirtatious) or Cabernet's (as complex but not as hedonistic).

Given the array of climates in which it is grown, Syrah is otherwise hard to generalise about. In Collines Rhodaniennes, you can find a 12% alcohol, lean, high acid, low-tannin wine with limited fruit. In Barossa, you can easily find 15% alcohol, low acid, full-bodied, jammy Syrah wines. This stylistic diversity is all the more reason to focus on the location and type of tannins.

Black pepper is the customary aroma note for the variety, although you will not find much of that in at least one classic region of origin: Barossa. I tend to find as much incense as black pepper in cooler climate examples, and I often look out for blue rather than black fruits in new world expressions.

Winemakers are increasingly adding stems to Syrah fermentations, to give the wine an additional spicy, aromatic lift. Finally, look out for the traditional co-fermentation with Viognier, evidenced in an even more lifted, floral perfume, and a hint of oiliness to the texture.

Confusions: Syrah can be confused with a range of full-bodied reds, especially with the Bordeaux varieties (including Malbec), but Syrah lacks the firm, tight tannin structure on the gums that characterises the Bordeaux varieties. Ribera del Duero Tempranillo is also a common confusion, but look out for the giveaway chalky tannins in the cheeks of that wine style. Zinfandel lacks the focused tannins of Syrah, while Tannat's tannins are less polished and integrated into the fruit.

Producers: see below under each region of origin.

Syrah by region

France

In France, Syrah can be a particularly 'wild' or 'untamed' variety in flavour terms: full of savoury, earthy notes. In most wines, fruit is at the front, aromatically and on the palate. But from the Northern Rhône, Syrah is one of the few varieties where fruit is pushed to the back; the savoury, earthy components tend to dominate the foreground (other examples include Madiran, Cahors, Bandol rouge and some Italian reds). French Syrah usually retains its acidity very well.

Northern Rhône Syrah arguably shows as much stylistic diversity in a small area here as Pinot Noir does in Burgundy or Cabernet Sauvignon does in the Médoc. The appellations of the northern Rhône may not be as famous as those others, but the terroir expression is brilliant and indisputable.

Qualitatively, the best wines in the northern Rhône come from the big three: Côte Rôtie in the north, Hermitage and the smaller Cornas in the south. St. Joseph generally shows more complexity than Crozes Hermitage, but both are a step down in complexity and ageworthiness from the big three appellations (with a couple of producers as noble exceptions).

Côte Rôtie: the single vineyard 'LaLa' wines of Guigal have confused us about the true identity of Côte Rôtie. Guigal's wines are huge, concentrated, heavily oaked and take decades to show well (although they are spectacular when they do!). But the classical identity of Côte Rôtie could hardly be more different: a medium-bodied wine, elegant, and aromatically sophisticated with a floral, violet perfume (enhanced by frequent co-fermentation with a little Viognier); delicate and refined. Côte Rôtie is the Pinot Noir of the northern Rhône and the most purely *beautiful* wine of the region. **Producers**: Guigal (Brune et Blonde bottling), Georges Vernay, René Rostaing, Levet, Jamet.

Hermitage: Hermitage gives intensely aromatic wines of saturated colour, with massive concentration and huge tannin structure when young, although as they age, they become more balanced and elegant in all but the hottest vintages. This is indisputably one of France's most long-lived wines and shows layers of flavour which require decades to emerge in full bloom. If you have identified the wine as Northern Rhône Syrah, selecting this appellation should be easy simply by the concentration and authority of the wine. **Producers**: JL Chave (including 'Selection' bottling), Chapoutier, Jaboulet, Marc Sorrel.

St. Joseph: in St. Joseph, wines vary from light and fruity to much more structured and dense. St. Joseph is never as powerful as Hermitage across the river, however, and shows less breadth than Cornas. It displays varietal Syrah characteristics (freshness, balance and black pepper notes) very transparently — more so than any other northern Rhône appellation. It is not usually as rustic as Crozes; St. Joseph is the more refined of the two, showing precision and clarity of flavour. **Producers**: JL Chave, Delas, Coursodon, Faury, Gonon (rare and expensive).

Crozes Hermitage: Crozes is denser than St. Joseph; more powerful and brawny, like Hermitage which it surrounds. But it lacks the elegance of St. Joseph and instead tends to be a touch rustic and earthy. **Producers**: Alain Graillot, Gilles Robin, Thalabert (Jaboulet), Delas.

Cornas: Cornas does not show the sheer mass and tannic superstructure of Hermitage, but it is nonetheless a powerful, brooding wine that needs considerable time to unfurl. When it does, it can display a spectacular floral (violets) perfume akin to Côte Rôtie but is considerably 'wilder' and more untamed, showing gamey, earthy notes. **Producers**: Clape, Domaine du Tunnel, Guillaume Gilles, Allemand.

New Zealand

There are some excellent, cool-climate Syrah wines emerging from Hawkes Bay. These tend to show only moderate alcohol, medium body, firm acidity and strong varietal characteristics in flavour terms, with prominent black pepper notes. Distinguishing these wines from the Northern Rhône can be tricky but focus on whether the wine is fruit-led (New Zealand) or more earthy (France). **Producers**: Craggy Range, Trinity Hill, Elephant Hill, Te Mata (Hawke's Bay).

Australia

The classic Shiraz origin is, of course, Barossa (and, to a lesser extent, McLaren Vale). Although the style here has been reined in a lot since its blockbuster days, these wines remain full-bodied, very concentrated, with high alcohol, ripe tannins and plush, velvety fruit. The fact that both fruit and tannin are so ripe means that the texture as a whole is plush and seamless. Many Barossa wines have a strong blueberry note and some are still aged in American oak. Overripe examples can be jammy or even syrupy. **Producers**: John Duval, Penfolds, Torbreck, d'Arenberg, Yalumba, Wirra Wirra (Barossa and McLaren Vale).

Outside Barossa, in regions such as Yarra Valley, Eden Valley, Canberra and various other regions in Western Australia, South Australia, Victoria and New South Wales, Shiraz shows more restraint. While still full bodied, these wines can show a more lifted, floral perfume (rather than just intense dark fruits) and elegance. The velvety smooth texture remains. In some regions, you may find the aromatic funkiness of whole cluster fermentation techniques. **Producers**: Leeuwin, Howard Park (Western Australia); Tahbilk, Mount Langi Ghiran, Fowles (Victoria); Shaw and Smith (South Australia); Tyrrell's (New South Wales).

Chile

Chilean Syrah is not a big category but is identifiable because it plays so true to Chilean type. That is, it is usually (not always) the lighter Syrah rather than the powerful Shiraz style; with a medium body, high acidity, moderate tannins and a delicate, floral aromatic spectrum. **Producers**: Montes (Colchagua); Errázuriz (Aconcagua); Concha y Toro (Central Valley).

USA

California: Syrah is being produced increasingly in California and mostly hews pretty closely to American winemaking styles. That is, look out for evident winemaking, either through a generous ripeness and use of new oak, or through use of stems in the increasingly numerous cooler-climate styles. The fruit always has a sunny ripeness to it although acidity and aromatics typical of the variety are usually well preserved. **Producers**: Ramey, Arnot-Roberts, Radio-Coteau (Sonoma Coast); Qupé, Piedrasassi (Santa Maria).

In **Washington**, some blockbuster styles are produced *à la* Hermitage – intensely concentrated, dark-fruited wines with huge tannin levels and often plenty of new oak. The best examples showcase Syrah's complex perfume, especially when co-fermented with Viognier. **Producers**: Reynvaan, Gramercy Cellars, Rasa (Walla Walla); Hedges (Red Mountain); Betz (various).

Grenache

Location of tannin: everywhere

Type of tannin: sticky, diffuse, gangly

Level of tannin: moderate

Construction: loose-knit tannins enveloped in rich fruit

Notes: Varietally labelled Grenache is produced in fewer geographic origins than the previously discussed four red varieties, but it is a very significant variety in the Rhône. The variety makes up the majority of most blends from the Côtes du Rhône — the second largest appellation in France, after Bordeaux.

Grenache is a little unusual for a wine of this weight, in that tannin is clearly not its focal point, nor is the tannin structure. Indeed, the tannin structure lacks an obvious shape or location in the mouth where the tannins are perceived.

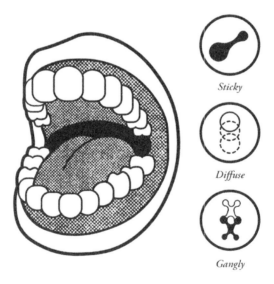

Sticky

Diffuse

Gangly

The Bordeaux varieties and Syrah have quite 'well-behaved,' predictable, and easy-to-understand tannin structures. Grenache does not. Grenache tannins are undisciplined and felt all over the palate. They are loose-knit and diffuse (or 'jangly'); they supply what I call 'structureless structure.' That means that while they are certainly present, they do not give much shape to the wine. Implicitly, that is what we expect tannins to do; Grenache is an exception to the rule (Zinfandel is another).

Texturally, Grenache tannins are quite sticky (somewhat like Merlot, but the firm structure of Merlot offers a contrast to the rather shapeless Grenache). Grenache is an eminently rich, sweet-tasting variety and easily lapses into being syrupy or tasting of dried fruits if overripe (this is one reason why it is often blended with higher acid and more savoury-tasting varieties). In spite of the sweet fruit, European examples of Grenache finish dry.

If unblended, Grenache can have a very pale colour, although Priorat proves how even a small amount of other varieties quickly darkens the colour. Ripe examples can have a Seville orange flavour; other varieties, when very ripe, can do too, but I see this curious syndrome more often in Grenache than in any other variety. Acidity is soft and usually only moderate in level. Grenache oxidises rather quickly.

At its finest, Grenache makes a rich, round wine, displaying a Pinot Noir-like purity of ripe red fruit, along with complex herbal and gamey notes. This combination of ripeness and dryness makes it a quintessential Mediterranean variety. Unfortunately, climate change is rendering it increasingly difficult to manage, and hot summers can produce very alcoholic wines. Some of the most exciting Grenache wines at present come from old vines or cooler sites at altitude, such as those in the Gredos mountains of Spain.

Confusions: the sweet-tasting fruit and only moderate tannins limit the number of confusions available for Grenache. Non-European Pinot Noir, for example from Sonoma, is a more understandable confusion than it might sound! But European Grenache should have a dry or savoury component. Outside Europe, Grenache should be a bigger wine all around than Pinot Noir. Grenache has more body and alcohol and less acidity than Gamay; additionally, if Gamay has a subtle dark minerality underlying the wine, Grenache is more spicy or herbal.

Producers: see below under each region of origin.

Grenache by Region

Côtes du Rhône: these inexpensive wines can be quite hard to identify because they are so generic. They are very 'standard issue' red French wines. The way I think about them is with comparison to AC Bordeaux wines. If AC Bordeaux are quintessential dry French reds, Côtes du Rhône are fruity French reds that walk the tightrope between being sweet and savoury. They are medium bodied, with moderate alcohol and firm but unobtrusive acidity. They show plenty of mid-palate sweet red fruits from the Grenache, while structure usually comes from the Syrah. A hint of spiciness or earthiness is also typical. Expect wines with a village name appended to show additional structure, complexity and ageworthiness. **Producers:** almost any producer of Châteauneuf-du-Pape or the other southern Rhône villages will also make a Côtes du Rhône. Classic Grenache-led examples are available from Perrin, Autard and Delas. Note that two of the best Côtes du Rhônes are Syrah-led: Guigal and St. Cosme.

Châteauneuf-du-Pape: a lot here depends on the blend. The glorious 100% Grenache wines from Bonneau or Rayas are, unfortunately, outliers. Those wines are perhaps the purest expressions of Grenache anywhere: pale colour; spicy, garrigue, herbal aromatics; a full body with high alcohol and with sweet red fruits expressed in a limpid purity of flavour.

More 'standard' Châteauneuf blended with Syrah, Mourvèdre, or the other permitted varieties tends to have a deeper colour and a more savoury flavour profile with less clearly etched fruit flavours. In all cases, the tannins of Châteauneuf, even while diffuse, are quite firm when young. **Producers**: Vieux Télégraphe, St. Préfert, Charvin, Pégau.

Gigondas/Vacqueyras: these are the most complex and ageworthy of the southern Rhône villages. **Gigondas** is really a mini-Châteauneuf, a classic Grenache/Syrah 'ripe but dry' blend just lacking some of the complexity and concentration of Châteauneuf. **Vacqueyras** importantly tends to use more Mourvèdre, giving a less sweet-tasting and more earthy, gamey style, as well as slightly firmer and more prominent tannins. If Gigondas is polished, Vacqueyras can be a touch more rugged. Both can have slightly lower alcohol than Châteauneuf (14-14.5% rather than 14.5-15%+) and tend to be more open – aromatically and in approachability of tannins – when young. **Producers**: St. Cosme, Bouïssière, Perrin, Pallières, des Tours, Grapillon d'Or, Montirius.

Spain

Priorat: although producers here are making more restrained styles now than 10 to 15 years ago, these are still among Europe's biggest wines. The Garnacha here is almost always blended with Cariñena (Carignan), which supplies much-needed acidity as well as tannin. Priorat can possess huge tannin structure – much more than the southern Rhône – along with a deeper colour and darker, more concentrated fruit flavours. Tar and slatey mineral are other common flavour notes. Sometimes Priorat can flirt with oxidation on the nose; the super-ripe fruit is in danger of losing its freshness and drying out (becoming maderised, nutty and tired). **Producers:** Álvaro Palacios, Mas Doix, Terroir al Límit, Mas d'en Gil.

Neighbouring **Montsant** is a mini-Priorat: stylistically similar, but with less of everything: colour, aromas, complexity, depth and tannins. **Producers:** Venus la Universal, Acústic.

The sea of Garnacha made in less premium regions of Spain tends to be brightly red-fruited, sweet tasting, supple and medium bodied.

Australia

On the sandy soils of McLaren Vale (and in some locations in Barossa), Grenache is a great Châteauneuf lookalike, with a pale colour and great purity and detail of flavour. What distinguishes it from French examples is the sweet, sometimes syrupy, finish which reveals its warmer new world origins. Although only representing a small proportion of Australia's plantings, Grenache seems to have a bright future in the country, in a deliciously lucid, purely-fruited style. **Producers:** Yangarra, Thistledown, SC Pannell (McLaren Vale).

Cabernet Franc

Location of tannin: gums

Type of tannin: grippy, grainy

Level of tannin: moderate

Construction: fresh acidity and textured tannins temper bright fruit

Notes: While many of us naturally think of the Loire when it comes to Cabernet Franc, it can be more helpful to focus on its identity as a Bordeaux variety. In common with Cabernet and Merlot, it has grainy, occasionally stalky tannins which grip the gums. Tannin levels tend to be moderate but occasionally feel pronounced because, like Cabernet Sauvignon, Cabernet Franc can lack fruit in the middle of the mouth.

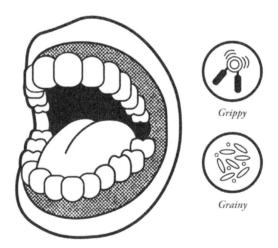

Grippy

Grainy

Cabernet Franc usually preserves its acidity very well and shows savoury red fruits and a strong aromatic profile, traditionally rather herbaceous in the Loire. But climate change has allowed easier ripening of Loire Cabernet Franc, such that the weedy, light-bodied, herbaceous reds of yore are increasingly rare. Today, more common are supple, medium-bodied, fresh reds with good fruit concentration and ripe red fruit flavours.

In the Loire, Chinon and Bourgueil and are the most important appellations, of which Chinon shows fresh, juicy fruit and Bourgueil tends to be more tannic and brooding. (As an aside, I have often made an unusual tasting note for Loire Cabernet Franc: on the nose, there is a sensation of static electricity, like when you rub a wool sweater. It is more a texture than an aroma, and it seems to float above the glass. This one may be personal just to me!).

At the very best Right Bank Bordeaux châteaux (Lafleur, Cheval Blanc, Vieux Château Certan), Cabernet Franc's presence in the blend is revealed by warm spice and tea aromas alongside an intricate, lattice-like web of finely detailed flavours. Outside France, it adds acidity to Super Tuscan blends and is also a popular variety in cool-climate regions in the northeast of the USA and in Canada. In Argentina, it can produce medium-bodied, leafy wines, but also very powerful, concentrated styles a far cry from the Loire and more like the country's signature Malbec.

Confusions: Cabernet Franc's less high quality (and less powerful) tannins minimise confusion with Cabernet Sauvignon. Merlot shows more mid-palate fruit. Cabernet Franc lacks the generous, supple fruitiness of Beaujolais. Mencia's tannins are felt in the cheeks rather than on the gums.

Producers: Bernard Baudry, Charles Joguet (Chinon); Domaine de la Butte, Yannick Amirault (Bourgueil).

Malbec

Location of tannin: gums, jaw

Type of tannin: grippy, grainy

Level of tannin: high

Construction: dense fruit framed by powerful, grainy tannins

Notes: The success of Argentinian Malbec has obscured the fact that this, too, is a Bordeaux variety. And once more, that is the key to identifying Malbec. Malbec's powerful tannins are – you guessed it! – grainy and felt on the gums. The best comparison among the other Bordeaux varieties is with Cabernet Sauvignon, thanks to the power and density of the tannins. But the difference is that Malbec tannins are more blocky and square rather than linear and directional like Cabernet's. They are more rustic than those of Cabernet or Merlot, meaning they lack a little polish and elegance.

We can also add some additional detail about where the tannins are felt. Rather than just being felt generically on the gums, Malbec tannins are felt on the hinge of the jaw specifically. This is why I call Malbec the 'lockjaw' variety: leave the wine on the palate too long, and it is hard to unstick your jaw and open your mouth again.

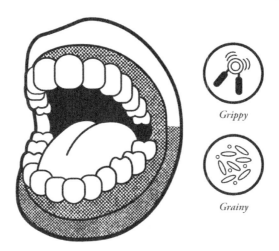

Grippy

Grainy

Malbec has a deeper, often more purple, colour than the other Bordeaux varieties. Another distinctive characteristic is the sweet/savoury confusion expressed in the variety. On the nose, Malbec smells quite sweet, often with a raspberry note (unusual because in a wine of this power you expect exclusively black fruits). But the wine finishes very dry, often with a prominent tobacco note or even a meaty quality. 'Starts sweet, finishes dry' (or 'sweet and sour') is an unusual description for a new world wine (note that Cahors examples can be less sweet to start than those from Argentina), and may help explain some of its huge commercial success: it has something for everyone.

In Cahors, Malbec looks more similar to Bordeaux varieties than anything else: built on powerful tannins, moderate acidity and dry, savoury fruit, with a long ageing potential. Even entry-level wines can take five or more years for the tannins to soften, unless they are made in an early-drinking international style (the name of the variety on the label is the usual giveaway for this type).

Confusions: Malbec's tannins are less directional than Cabernet's. It shows similar mid-palate fruit density to Merlot, but the tannins do not quite show the same quality, and the fruit is less velvety and supple. Carmenère is a better guess but usually Malbec is a bigger, more tannic wine all around and lacks Carmenère's perceptible acidity (at least when Carmenère is grown in Chile). Syrah shows a similarly deep colour but lacks Malbec's 'lockjaw' tannins.

Producers: Catena, Zuccardi, Norton, Altos Las Hormigas, Colomé, Diamandes (Argentina); Coutale, Chambert, Lagrézette (Cahors).

Carmenère

Location of tannin: gums

Type of tannin: powerful, grainy

Level of tannin: high

Construction: glossy fruit overlays a powerful tannin structure

Notes: Completing our survey of sometime Bordeaux varieties, Carmenère is today almost exclusively grown in Chile. There, it makes inky-coloured, powerfully-structured wines which are almost always herbaceous. The variety is naturally herbaceous-tasting, and when Chile's native greenness is added, you are piling green on green. The dark fruit often has an attractive glossy quality to it which contrasts with the grainy quality of the tannins. Outside Chile, some Carmenère is grown by producers such as Inama in the Veneto.

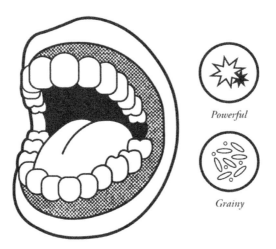

Powerful

Grainy

Confusions: Chilean Carmenère is more herbaceous than Chilean Cabernet Sauvignon as well as showing coarser tannins, a rounder body and sweeter tasting fruit (to the point of being syrupy). Carmenère is also more herbaceous than Malbec.

Producers: Santa Rita, Concha y Toro, Errázuriz.

Gamay

Location of tannin: gums

Type of tannin: chalky

Level of tannin: moderate

Construction: juicy fruit highlighted by acidity, tannins, cool minerality and a dry finish

Notes: Gamay from Beaujolais is a wine that is missed surprisingly often by tasters. Structurally, Gamay has low to moderate levels of ripe, chalky tannins, felt on the gums. In spite of the wine's juicy fruitiness, its excellent acidity, tannins and dry finish create an attractive sense of balance. The best examples from the cru villages also offer a cool, rocky, slatey minerality at the heart of the wine and an excellent floral and spicy perfume. Beaujolais is a wine of contrasts, poised between its generous fruit and its dry, savoury components.

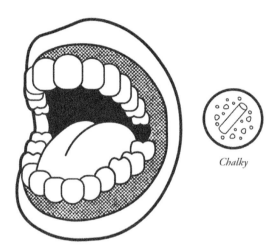

Chalky

Cru Beaujolais is generally vinified in the same traditional way as Burgundy, rather than with the use of any semi-carbonic maceration (which gives the bubble gum, banana aromas and tends to make light, simple wines). The most structured villages are Morgon, Chénas, Brouilly and Moulin à Vent, with Fleurie the most popular of the lighter, more aromatic crus.

Confusions: Pinot Noir is the most obvious confusion, thanks to the light/mid-weight body and juicy fruit. However, the fruit in Gamay is marginally sweeter-tasting than Pinot's, even while the variety shows a similar bright colour and firm acidity. Gamay is round or spherical in the mouth (the generous, rich fruit coats all corners of the mouth), while Pinot Noir is more upwards focused (see Pinot Noir).

Thanks to Gamay's sweet fruit profile, Grenache can be a confusion. Gamay's acidity is higher, though, and its tannins more structured than Grenache's loose knit, diffuse tannins. Gamay tannins give more shape to the wine. Additionally, alcohol levels should be one percent lower in Beaujolais than in wines from the southern Rhône, with the attendant effects on the wine's weight: even cru Beaujolais is rarely more than medium-bodied. In flavour terms, Beaujolais is less 'wild' than Grenache and altogether lacks the garrigue herb of a good southern Rhône Grenache.

Gamay is fruitier than the more savoury Blaufränkisch and Syrah. Dolcetto is slightly darker both in colour and in fruit profile, and it finishes more savoury (even bitter) in spite of its sweet fruit.

Producers: Jean-Paul Brun, Marcel Lapierre, Thivin, Alain Coudert/Clos de la Roilette, Julien Sunier (Beaujolais).

Mourvèdre

Location of tannin: gums

Type of tannin: heavy, coarse

Level of tannin: high

Construction: rich Mediterranean fruit balanced by powerful tannins and earthy dryness

Notes: This is the variety of Bandol and an important blending partner of southern Rhône reds. Mourvèdre is a particularly useful blending variety since it brings a savoury, dry, earthy quality to the otherwise rich, sweet-tasting Grenache. It adds structure, freshness and earthiness to Rhône blends and also ripens at lower alcohol levels than Grenache.

In Bandol, Mourvèdre wines are full-bodied and concentrated, with powerful, slightly rustic tannins felt on the gums, like Bordeaux varieties. The difference from the Bordeaux varieties is the texture of Mourvèdre's tannins, which are coarser than Bordeaux tannins. Look out also for a distinctive black olive note.

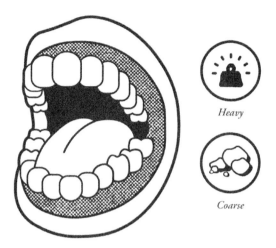

Heavy

Coarse

In Spain, in Jumilla and Yecla, Mourvèdre (there called Monastrell) makes Spain's most savoury, dry, full-bodied red wine. The tannins can be huge and rustic and make the mid-palate fruit feel rather lightweight by comparison. Look for the unusual combination of intense fruit ripeness offset by dryness, in the form of moderate acidity and a chalky texture (so common in wines grown on limestone soils). Whether it is grown in France or Spain, Mourvèdre is a very Mediterranean wine, combining ripe fruit with a dry finish.

Confusions: Mourvèdre shows riper, softer fruit than Tannat and Carignan, and more tannin and freshness than Grenache.

Producers: Tempier, Pibarnon, Pradeaux (Bandol); Juan Gil, Casa Castillo (Jumilla).

Carignan

Location of tannin: gums

Type of tannin: grainy

Level of tannin: high

Construction: dry, concentrated fruit buttressed by powerful tannins, high acidity and a savoury finish

Notes: Varietal Carignan wines are made in Spain, Chile and Languedoc-Roussillon, although in the latter, it is more common to see the variety as a blending component (e.g. Corbières). Carignan (Mazuelo or Cariñena in Spain) requires some work to tame its powerful tannins, but winemakers are then rewarded by a red that retains admirable freshness and savoury character in warm to hot climates. When unblended, it can appear a little austere thanks to its dryness (of fruit, tannins, finish), but careful handling or bottle age will mitigate this.

Carignan shows high acidity, concentrated, red and black fruits and spice flavours, and powerful tannins felt on the gums. The finish of the wine can be notably earthy or savoury. Some winemakers are trying now to tame the tannins by using carbonic maceration resulting in light, fruity styles. In blends Carignan is useful for contributing acidity, structure and colour.

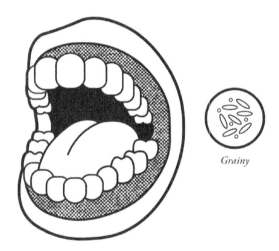

Grainy

Confusions: Carignan is more savoury and earthy than Grenache or Tempranillo; Mourvèdre would be a better Mediterranean confusion for its earthiness and grippy tannins. But Mourvèdre's fruit is slightly sweeter-tasting and lacks any tannic bitterness on the finish.

Carignan should not be confused with Cinsaut, the other broadly planted blending variety of southern France. Cinsaut by contrast offers ample, simple, juicy fruit, some perfume and low tannins.

Producers: Domaine of the Bee, Domaine Jones (Languedoc-Rousillon); Mas Doix (Priorat); de Martino, Undurraga (Maule).

Tannat

Location of tannin: gums

Type of tannin: powerful, dry, dripping

Level of tannin: high

Construction: dense fruit and powerful tannins create a structured, savoury red

Notes: In Madiran, Tannat makes some of France's most powerful red wines; even inexpensive examples need years in bottle for the tannins to become approachable. The tannins are so heavy that they feel as if they are dripping off the upper gums, their weight insupportable. Madiran is a hearty, rustic wine in the best sense: meaty, earthy and gamey, especially with age; here we are a long way from polished Bordeaux. In Uruguay, Tannat shows good acidity and the same density of fruit and tannins, although sometimes winemakers use techniques such as micro-oxygenation to soften the tannins.

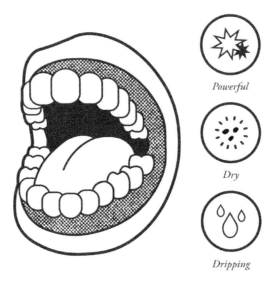

Powerful

Dry

Dripping

Confusions: Tannat has more tannin than Malbec, and in France is a more 'wild,' gamey, earthy wine than the more traditional Bordeaux-profiled Malbec. Tannat has more solidity all around than the richer, softer-fruited Mediterranean Mourvèdre. Carignan's tannins lack the heavy, 'dripping' sensation exhibited by those of Tannat.

Producers: Bouscassé, Montus (Madiran); Garzón (Uruguay).

Blaufränkisch

Location of tannin: gums, rear gums

Type of tannin: chalky, grainy

Level of tannin: moderate

Construction: ripe, velvety fruit grounded by firm structure and earthy flavour notes

Notes: If Austria has a signature red variety, this is it. Medium bodied, Blaufränkisch shows chalky, grainy tannins on the gums which in some cases can even be rugged or rustic. Far from being a flimsy, light variety, the structure here is firm and prominent, contributing to a substantial wine. Not for nothing is it often aged in oak.

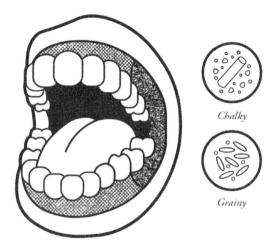

Chalky

Grainy

The acidity is moderate to high and shows the distinctive Austrian tanginess (an Austrian signature – see Grüner Veltliner and Riesling). This tanginess is underscored by the spice, smoke, incense and black pepper notes common to the variety. Blaufränkisch has a Malbec-like habit of showing concentrated dark or blue fruit, but with a red fruit and floral top note. These flavour complexities emerge even at relatively low alcohol levels (13% or less).

In spite of the supple, velvety fruit, Blaufränkisch makes an elementally dry, savoury wine thanks to the emphasis on the acidity, the peppery, tangy character and the firm, dry tannins.

Confusions: Compared to Gamay's generous fruitiness, Blaufränkisch is more earthy and spicy; Pinot Noir is silkier and airier rather than earthy. Austrian Zweigelt shows a paler colour, a lighter body, higher acidity and less concentration than Blaufränkisch, although may still show peppery notes. Zweigelt has attractive lifted floral and spice aromas. St. Laurent is aromatic and velvety, like Pinot, but neither it nor Zweigelt show Blaufränkisch's depth and concentration.

Producers: Moric, Hans and Anita Nittnaus, Paul Achs (Burgenland).

Tempranillo

Location of tannin: cheeks

Type of tannin: chalky

Level of tannin: moderate

Construction: chalky tannins, fresh acidity and a savoury core underpin supple fruit

Notes: Spain's signature variety is produced in a variety of styles, but fortunately for the taster, has a range of consistent attributes. As ever, the truth is in the tannins, and Tempranillo's are distinctive for two reasons: their texture and location.

Tempranillo has chalky tannins which are felt in the cheeks. Chalky tannins are unusual and noteworthy. Northern Rhône Syrah can sometimes show chalky tannins, but there, the location of the tannins is on the tongue. Here, it is not on the gums; it is very specifically the cheeks. After a few seconds on the palate, Tempranillo leaves a chalk dust sensation in the cheeks.

Chalkiness seems to be associated with limestone soils, the best example among red wine regions being St. Emilion, whose wines often finish chalky. But that is the texture of the fruit, not of the tannins. Here, the chalkiness refers to the tannins alone. This is another two-texture wine (see Merlot), where the fruit has a different texture than the tannins: Tempranillo's fruit is seamless and elegant, sometimes velvety, but the tannins are chalky.

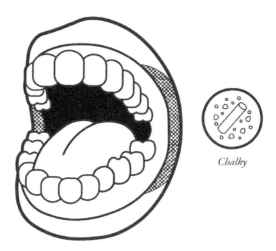

Chalky

Tempranillo usually retains its acidity well, ensuring that even the warmest-climate examples from Ribera del Duero are fresh. In traditional examples of Rioja, the acidity can assume a 'pixelated' quality — it shines through the fruit like little pinpricks of light.

Examples from Rioja also show moderate levels of tannin, supple red rather than black fruits, and a dark, mineral, umami core which emerges with age. Winemaking can range from extremely traditional (years in older French and American oak) to modern (up to 18 months in new French barriques). Rioja often shows a 'sweet and sour' sensation given by the combination of sweet tasting oak with the savoury fruit and acidity.

More modern winemaking styles tend to be fuller-bodied, while classical Rioja is only medium bodied. Rioja rarely exceeds 14% alcohol. If it is not blended with too much Garnacha (or, in Ribera, with the Bordeaux varieties), Rioja can be relatively light-coloured.

From Ribera del Duero (and Toro), expect a powerful, concentrated, full bodied, dark-fruited wine often aged in new oak. Stylistically, these are a long way from the traditional examples of Rioja and could be confused with numerous 'international style' wines from around the world. But Tempranillo's distinctive tannins are the clue here – again look out for chalkiness in the cheeks.

Lesser examples of Tempranillo from around Spain show simple red fruit flavours and moderate acidity and alcohol. These wines have less fruit but more freshness than their Garnacha equivalents.

Confusions: Rioja (and Ribera) could be confused for Bordeaux, but lack the 'square,' grippy tannins felt on the gums. Syrah has more tannin emphasis on the tongue (middle) than the cheeks (edge of the mouth). More international, fruit-driven, powerful styles of Tempranillo from Ribera del Duero can be confused with Malbec, non-European Cabernet Sauvignon or numerous other powerful wines, but the chalky tannins in the cheeks are the all-important distinguishing feature.

Producers: CVNE, Muga, López de Heredia, Beronia, Bideona (Rioja); Pesquera, Hacienda Monasterio, Pago de los Capellanes (Ribera del Duero).

Mencia

Location of tannin: cheeks

Type of tannin: chalky

Level of tannin: moderate

Construction: velvety fruit contrasts with chalky tannins and a dry finish

Notes: Mencia is similar in many respects to Tempranillo, with moderate, firm, chalky tannins felt in the cheeks (and to a lesser extent the gums). However, it diverges from Tempranillo in the texture of the fruit. Mencia's fruit is particularly soft and velvety and marks a strong contrast to the chalky tannins. Mencia is usually only medium-bodied, with plenty of dark fruit flavours; acidity is medium to high, although Mencia is sometimes acidified in Bierzo. Perhaps unexpected after the easy-going fruit is the serious, savoury finish; occasionally featuring green olive, meaty or smoky notes.

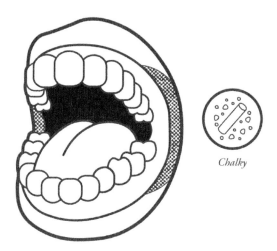

Chalky

Confusions: A natural confusion for Mencia is Right Bank Bordeaux, where Merlot can give the velvety fruit texture, and St. Emilion the limestone chalkiness. Mencia can even display a spicy, herbal, peppery note reminiscent of Cabernet Franc or Syrah. But the tannins are felt in the wrong place for both of those varieties — in the cheeks rather than exclusively on the gums (Bordeaux) or on the tongue (Syrah). Mencia usually shows lighter and less dense fruit than Syrah. It has a richer fruit texture than Tempranillo and a slightly more funky, savoury flavour profile.

Producers: Algueira, Guímaro (Ribeira Sacra); Raúl Pérez, Descendientes de J. Palacios (Bierzo).

Xinomavro

Location of tannin: rear gums

Type of tannin: grippy, grainy

Level of tannin: moderate

Construction: high acidity and rugged tannins contrast with soft fruit

Notes: Xinomavro's most obvious confusion is with Nebbiolo, which tells you a lot about the quality and complexity of this variety. Xinomavro gives an aromatic wine, pale coloured, with moderate (sometimes high) levels of grippy, grainy (occasionally astringent) tannin felt on the gums, especially the rear gums. It often shows high acidity and an herbal note. There is usually sufficient (but not generous) soft, sweet-tasting red fruit to ensure that neither tannins nor acidity feel excessive.

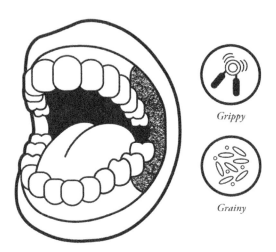

Grippy

Grainy

Confusions: The difference from Nebbiolo is ripeness – the fruit here is sweeter and more concentrated on the mid palate, and the body fuller and rounder. The tannins can be a touch rougher than Nebbiolo's more polished ('long grain') tannins. Xinomavro is usually lighter in colour than Aglianico, and it lacks Aglianico's aromatic funkiness (incense, meatiness etc) in favour of a more common red fruited and floral profile.

Producers: Alpha, Kir-Yianni (Amyndeo); Thymiopoulos (Naoussa).

Saperavi

Location of tannin: gums

Type of tannin: sticky, grainy

Level of tannin: moderate

Construction: generous fruit balanced by savoury dryness and tartness

Notes: Georgia's great red variety deserves our attention given the increasingly fine wines emerging from the country. Saperavi is distinctive and rendered even more so when made in the traditional qvevri clay vessels which seem to draw out all the peculiarities of the variety.

Look for: a deep colour, sticky, grainy tannins on the gums, an overlay of rich, juicy, dark berry fruit and prominent, high acidity. The finish is conspicuously dry; because of the high acidity, it can even be tart. Saperavi from Georgia often exhibits a funky, meaty flavour note, compounding the overall savoury quality of the variety.

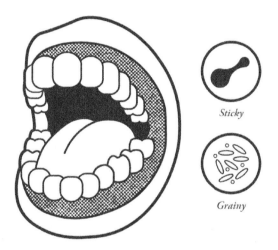

Sticky

Grainy

Confusions: Many dry European reds could be confusions, including the Bordeaux varieties, or perhaps some Italian reds. But the aggressive dryness of Saperavi's finish and tart acidity would be unusual even for Bordeaux. There is too much mid-palate generosity of fruit for most Italian wines. Saperavi's funky, meaty note is also hard to imagine in most more commonly seen varieties.

Producers: Askaneli Brothers, Orgo, Dakishvili (Georgia); Dr. Konstantin Frank (Finger Lakes, New York).

Touriga Nacional blends

Location of tannin: gums

Type of tannin: grippy

Level of tannin: high

Construction: fruit retreats in the face of a powerful, dry structure

Notes: Dry red wines from the Douro Valley are almost always blends, but Touriga Nacional often predominates. Predictably from this hot climate, these wines are full-bodied, and their grippy tannins are felt on the gums. The key to identifying this wine style, though, rests on two features.

First, the wines are ripe but dry. With all the concentrated fruit packed in there, you might expect some sweetness, but no — these wines are completely dry (possibly taking you away from sweeter-tasting Mediterranean wines from Spain or France).

Second, the wines tend to lack mid-palate concentration. In wines of this scale, mid palate should be a given. But in Touriga blends, the mid-palate fruit is not as dense as expected and plays a secondary role to the structure. Finally, in spite of the climate, the grapes that go into these wines preserve their acidity very well.

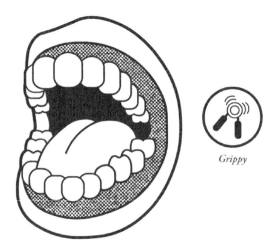

Grippy

Confusions: The 'ripe but dry' character of these wines distinguishes them from any wine containing sweet-fruited Grenache. They show more blocky tannin and fruit than the linear, streamlined Cabernet Sauvignon. Touriga-led wines possess too much colour and density to be confused with Italian varieties. Other indigenous Portuguese varieties such as Baga show a similarly firm tannin structure and intense dryness, in spite of their fruit, but they lack the floral perfume of Touriga Nacional.

Producers: Casa Ferreirinha, Chryseia, Quinta do Crasto, Niepoort, Quinta do Noval, Transdouro Express (Douro).

Zinfandel

Location of tannin: everywhere

Type of tannin: velvety, chewy, loose knit, diffuse

Level of tannin: moderate

Construction: sweet-tasting fruit, rich texture and ample tannin create an intense wine

Notes: Yes, this is the same variety as Primitivo, but when Zinfandel comes from the US, the variety behaves quite differently in the glass than it does in Italy. Zinfandel's tannins are similar to those of Grenache in that, while moderate or even high in quantity, they offer 'structureless structure' – they can be powerful, and are felt all over the palate, but they are loose knit and diffuse. They give very little sense of architecture or shape to the wine.

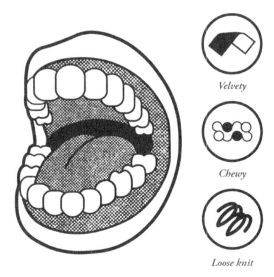

Velvety

Chewy

Loose knit

Zinfandel is a full-bodied, rich, sweet-tasting, high-alcohol wine which unusually shows both red and black fruits on the nose, or even ripe and unripe notes simultaneously, thanks to the variety's tendency to achieve different ripeness levels within a single bunch. The fruit can be jammy and taste even riper than Grenache. But the sweetness is offset by a savoury tobacco note (also present in White Zinfandel). Zinfandel's fruit has a natural propensity for new oak – both French and, especially, American.

Confusions: Zinfandel has a deeper colour and more weight of fruit than almost all Grenache wines (the exception being Priorat, but Priorat's tannins are tighter than those of Zinfandel). Zinfandel shows less defined structure than the Bordeaux or Italian varieties (ironically!). It is sweeter than Syrah.

Producers: Ridge, Turley, Bedrock, Seghesio (California).

Pinotage

Location of tannin: gums, cheeks

Type of tannin: powerful, coarse

Level of tannin: high

Construction: brawny tannins and dense fruit in a savoury register

Notes: Pinotage has powerful Bordeaux-style tannins felt on the gums. The longer you hold the wine on your palate, the more the tannins seem to expand into the cheeks. Pinotage's tannins are more rugged, brawny and coarse than those of the Bordeaux varieties. Taming Pinotage's tannins is a big challenge for winemakers.

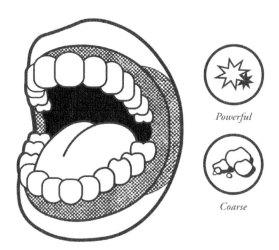

Powerful

Coarse

Pinotage classically makes a full-bodied, dark-fruited, concentrated, high alcohol, savoury wine, with an earthy smokiness and a dry finish. Some winemakers are experimenting with lighter, fresher versions, even some made with carbonic maceration.

Confusions: Various full-bodied international-style wines may be confusions, but look out for Pinotage's slightly unpolished tannins (compared to the Bordeaux varieties or Syrah) and its funky, meaty, smoky note not usually found in those well-known varieties.

Producers: Kanonkop, Kaapzicht, Beyerskloof (Stellenbosch).

Italian Red Varieties

Among the hundreds of indigenous red Italian varieties, I focus on those most commonly seen, presented in order from north to south. Please refer to the section on Italy, in Tasting for Region of Origin, for general characteristics of Italian reds.

Dolcetto

Location of tannin: gums

Type of tannin: grainy

Level of tannin: moderate

Construction: soft fruit and modest acidity contrast with grainy tannins

Notes: 'The little sweet one' is so-called because it is unusual among Italian red varieties for having only moderate levels of acidity, giving a 'sweet' taste (there are other suggested origins of the name, but this one makes such good sense, I am sticking with it!). The tannins are nonetheless moderate and grainy, meaning that this is no cocktail wine. Look out for a deep, often purple colour, 'sweet and sour' black fruit and liquorice flavours and a particularly soft, supple texture for an Italian variety. Dolcetto can finish with a little bitterness.

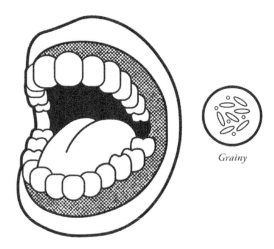

Grainy

Confusions: The sweet taste of the fruit eliminates confusion with many more savoury Italian varieties. It is more black-fruited than Valpolicella or Montepulciano but is still distinctly Italian with its grainy tannins on the gums. It lacks the power and density of Barbera.

Producers: B. Mascarello, G.B. Burlotto, G.D. Vajra, Vietti, Einaudi.

Barbera

Location of tannin: gums

Type of tannin: grainy, chalky

Level of tannin: moderate

Construction: richly fruited wine firmly structured by grainy tannins and acidity

Notes: Barbera is a wine of concentrated dark fruit and a moderate to full body, framed by moderate levels of grainy (sometimes chalky) tannins, felt on the gums. It has the trademark Italian high acidity. However, unlike many Italian reds, colour-wise, Barbera can show a rather deep colour – all the way to deep purple, depending on ripeness. In flavour terms, it tends towards dark (brambly) fruit rather than red.

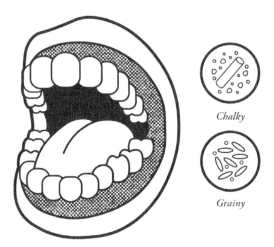

Chalky

Grainy

Barbera's depth of fruit and firm tannin structure means that it deserves more respect than it sometimes receives. While it may not always improve with age, it can certainly hold for ten or more years from the best producers, such as those listed below. Look out for high quality examples from Nizza, a new (2014) DOCG dedicated to this variety.

Confusions: The acidity and grainy tannin are enough to put you in Italy. Like Dolcetto, Barbera can show some bitterness on the finish, but has greater fruit concentration, tannin levels and a more rounded body than Dolcetto. It is a more structured and ambitious wine all around. Barbera has a deeper colour and more mid-palate fruit than Sangiovese or Aglianico. A Super Tuscan Bordeaux blend might be a better guess, but Barbera's tannins would be less polished than those.

Producers: Castello di Perno (Nizza); G.D. Vajra, Vietti, Cigliuti, Sottimano, Paolo Scavino, Bruno Giacosa (Alba).

Nebbiolo

Location of tannin: gums

Type of tannin: long-grained, sandy

Level of tannin: high

Construction: delicate, ethereal fruit floats on top of a powerful tannin structure

Notes: Nebbiolo, behaving as a typical Italian variety, is built on the twin pillars of acidity and tannin. Both can be among the highest of any red varieties. Nebbiolo's tannins, like Bordeaux tannins, are felt on the gums and texturally are sandy or grainy. The tannins – unlike those of the Bordeaux varieties – can be among the most astringent of all red varieties. Nebbiolo is almost always pale coloured, red-fruited, with a medium to full body and high alcohol. It frequently can lack mid-palate fruit, with the focal point instead being the tannins around the edge of the mouth.

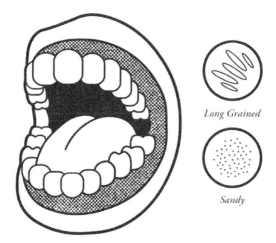

Long Grained

Sandy

The brilliance of Nebbiolo though, is obscured by that technical description. The vividness and delicacy of the variety's aromas and flavours combined with the powerful tannin structure creates one of the most unexpected juxtapositions in wine. In the best examples, the aromas seem to soar out of the glass, and the fruit dances on the palate, animated by the acidity. But the dry tannins, as well as the earthy, herbal, amaro flavours so characteristic of Italian reds, are much more 'of the earth.' In this sense, Nebbiolo occupies a liminal position, its head in the clouds, its feet firmly on earth. This poise is almost unique in the world of wine.

Valtellina and Gattinara make light to medium bodied styles with pretty aromatics. But the haunting aromas of great Barbaresco or Barolo are one of the variety's outstanding features.

Confusions: The most obvious confusion for Nebbiolo is Sangiovese. The best way of telling them apart is by the texture of the tannins. Although both show sandy or grainy tannins, Nebbiolo tannins are higher quality because they are longer-grained than Sangiovese tannins. Sangiovese tannins feel like little grains of tannin (like short-grained rice) while Nebbiolo tannins are long-grained (like long-grained rice) which gives a greater sleekness and elegance to them.

Nebbiolo has higher quality tannins than Aglianico. It is more similar to Nerello Mascalese, but Nerello usually lacks the delicacy and some of the complex perfume of Nebbiolo's fruit. Nebbiolo shows more finesse than Xinomavro.

Producers: Vietti, G.D. Vajra, Paolo Scavino, Brovia, Ceretto, Castello di Perno (Barolo); Cascina delle Rose, Produttori del Barbaresco, Ceretto, Marchesi di Gresy, Cigliuti (Barbaresco).

Nebbiolo by region: Barolo and Barbaresco

The great Nebbiolo wines of Barolo and Barbaresco are some of the world's most distinctive reds. The challenge for the wine student is to distinguish between them. Due to the huge stylistic diversity in winemaking throughout Piedmont, trying to establish which is which can be difficult to the point of being futile.

It is true that Barolo and Barbaresco have different ageing requirements: 18 months in oak for Barolo, only nine for Barbaresco, and three years' total ageing for Barolo as opposed to two for Barbaresco. That indicates that Barbaresco may be a less substantial, concentrated wine than Barolo, and may suggest that Barbaresco is less tannic.

In my tastings, I often (but not always) find Barbaresco to be just as tannic as Barolo, but I do find that Barbaresco seems to drink well a bit younger. So maybe it is a touch less concentrated, and the tannins are a little less dense.

Barbaresco is looser knit and open from the beginning; it can be extremely aromatic even when young, showing pure Nebbiolo class almost immediately. Of course, Barolo achieves all that – with time. Barbaresco *may* be the more elegant and less heavy of the two as many tasters say, but I prefer to look for aromatic lift and how easy the wine is to enjoy in its youth.

Corvina and the Valpolicella varieties

Location of tannin: gums

Type of tannin: chalky, dusty

Level of tannin: moderate

Construction: rich, juicy red fruit offset by acidity, chalky tannins and a dry finish

Notes: Note that Corvina is the dominant grape in Valpolicella blends; the other varieties are minor blending partners. Valpolicella is light to medium-bodied, shows juicy or even rich red fruit, low to moderate levels of chalky or dusty tannins felt on the gums, moderate to high acidity and moderate alcohol. In characteristically Italian fashion, Corvina has an herbal (anise/tarragon) edge and a dry finish. Better examples show excellent precision of fresh red fruits and a chalky finish.

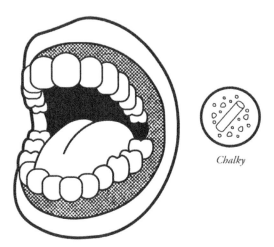

Chalky

The Ripasso process adds body, alcohol, depth and complexity of flavour, with a savoury, sometimes meaty quality and a chocolatey rich texture. But the best way of identifying Valpolicella Ripasso is by the singular notes given by the winemaking process. Look out for elevated levels of volatile acidity, detected by the aroma of nail polish remover, as well as a certain mustiness in more traditional examples.

Amarone is similar in style, but with greater influence of dried grapes. Amarone should be easy to spot for other reasons too: the massive tannic charge of the wines, a bitter finish and very high alcohol (15-17%). In addition, there is often a little (under 10g/l) residual sugar left in the wine, and a sensation of alcohol-derived sweetness (i.e., the high alcohol makes the wine taste sweeter than it really is). Amarone is probably the most powerful non-fortified wine commonly available, and it tastes like it.

Confusions: There are few wines that Amarone can be confused with thanks to its body, alcohol and tannins. Valpolicella could be confused with several other Italian varieties thanks to its high acidity, sour red cherry fruit and chalky/dusty tannins. But it is a little less high-toned than Chianti. It is red fruited rather than Dolcetto or Barbera's darker profile. The most likely confusion might be Montepulciano, but Montepulciano is more tart, more tannic and shows less supple, easy fruit.

Producers: Bertani (a fresher, lighter style of Amarone than most), Zenato, Bussola, Allegrini, Masi.

Sangiovese

Location of tannin: gums

Type of tannin: sandy, grainy

Level of tannin: moderate

Construction: sandy tannins, a dusty fruit texture and high acidity give a quintessentially Italian wine of texture and freshness

Notes: Sangiovese is one of the great Italian varieties, capable of displaying aromatic complexity, elegant fruit and considerable ageing potential. Sangiovese's capacity to express itself so differently in different terroirs is another reason that makes it compelling to wine lovers (see Sangiovese by region, below). In spite of regional differences, however, Sangiovese consistently shows sandy (sometimes grainy) tannins felt on the gums; tangy, high acidity; and a dusty, sour red fruit profile. This classically Italian profile makes Sangiovese (particularly Chianti) a quintessential Italian red.

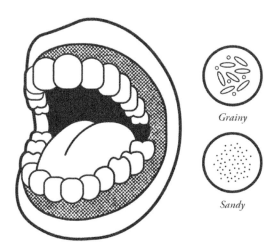

Grainy

Sandy

Confusions: Sangiovese is readily confused with Nebbiolo because they both share a pale to medium colour, medium to full body, an aromatic style and moderate to high levels of sandy tannins felt on the gums. What distinguishes them? As mentioned above (see Nebbiolo), Sangiovese tannins are not quite as high quality as Nebbiolo tannins. Sangiovese tannins are short-grained and can feel a little like sandpaper in young wines, but Nebbiolo tannins are longer-grained and more elegant.

In addition, the fruit has a different texture to Nebbiolo fruit. Sangiovese fruit has a distinctive dusty quality to it, which contrasts with the sandy tannins. Sangiovese often has more mid-palate fruit concentration than Nebbiolo, especially in Montalcino, as befits its more southern origin. The aromas of Sangiovese are usually a little less high-toned than Nebbiolo's.

Producers: see below under each region of origin.

Sangiovese by region

The Sangiovese of Tuscany has always been one of the world's great red varieties, but, for reasons best known to themselves, many Tuscan winemakers concealed that fact until quite recently. Excessive extraction, inappropriate inclusion of lesser blending varieties (including international varieties), ill-advised use of new oak: these techniques all contributed to obscuring the true glory of Sangiovese.

Thankfully, since about 2011, we appear to be in a new era, as the pendulum has swung away from extraction and towards finesse – a winemaking choice that suits this elegant variety so well. As a result, it is now easier to appreciate the distinctive qualities of the three principal growing regions: Chianti (Classico), Brunello di Montalcino and Vino Nobile di Montepulciano.

Chianti

I am grouping all the Chianti subzones into one here, although the following description applies most readily to the best of them: Chianti Classico. Chianti should be a medium-bodied wine (only full-bodied in particularly powerful Riserva/Gran Selezione versions, especially from the south of the zone), with high-toned aromatics and moderate, sandy tannins. Chianti's distinctly tangy acidity brings a brilliant vibrancy and energy to the wine.

What I particularly note in Chianti is its *dusty* texture – this is a good example of a wine where the texture of the tannins is different from the texture of the fruit. While the tannins are sandy, there is a distinctly dusty sensation left on the palate by the fruit. (I always imagine driving down a dusty vineyard track under the Tuscan sun).

With age, the tannins and acidity mellow to create a gentle, soft wine. The best non-Riserva Chianti approaches the condition of Burgundy in its lightness, aromatic beauty and lacy purity. **Producers:** Fontodi, Felsina, Castell in'Villa, Monsanto, Rocca di Montegrossi.

Brunello di Montalcino

The Brunello clone of Sangiovese grown in Montalcino, coupled with a warmer growing region, gives a different rendition of Sangiovese than Chianti's. Brunello is a more muscular, concentrated, full-bodied wine than Chianti; if Chianti is playful, Brunello can be a little stern. The high levels of tannin and concentration of fruit need considerably longer than Chianti to mellow. Anecdotally, I also often find a strong bay leaf or liquorice note in Brunello that only occasionally do I find in Chianti. **Producers:** Poggione, Val di Suga, Col d'Orcia, Baricci, La Magia, Lisini.

Vino Nobile di Montepulciano

Vino Nobile is a kind of rustic cross between Chianti and Brunello. Ultimately, it lacks the quality of either; it possesses neither the finesse of Chianti nor the authority of Brunello. But it does offer an aromatic profile similar to Chianti, and a concentration of fruit akin to Brunello. Vino Nobile's tannins are more rustic than either of the others, however, and the alcohol can be obtrusive. With a few exceptions from the best producers, Vino Nobile remains an everyday wine. **Producers:** Dei, Avignonesi, Boscarelli.

Montepulciano

Location of tannin: gums

Type of tannin: chalky, grainy

Level of tannin: moderate

Construction: generous mid-palate fruit shaped by chalky tannin and high acidity

Notes: Montepulciano (d'Abruzzo is the most commonly seen appellation) is another typical Italian red in many facets: high acidity, moderate chalky or grainy tannins felt on the gums and a sour red fruit flavour profile. It usually shows a rather deep colour and succulent, juicy mid-palate fruit – there is little of Nebbiolo or Chianti's occasional lightness here. Montepulciano is not as aromatic as either of those wines. Lesser Montepulciano wines (of which there are many) are light, fresh and simple.

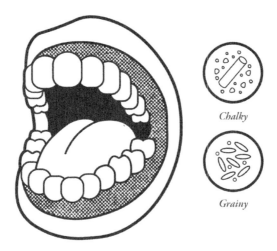

Chalky

Grainy

Confusions: Montepulciano d'Abruzzo is most readily confused with Chianti, particularly because of its dusty, sandy texture. But Montepulciano shows a deeper colour, greater fruit ripeness and more mid-palate concentration than Chianti usually does, albeit not at the level of Brunello. Sangiovese also shows a greater (and usually more attractive) perfume. The generous fruit can suggest Valpolicella, but Montepulciano shows more tannin and is a drier wine overall. Barbera is darker-fruited than Montepulciano.

Producers: Masciarelli, Tiberio, Pasetti, Torre dei Beati.

Aglianico

Location of tannin: gums

Type of tannin: sandy, coarse

Level of tannin: high

Construction: distinctive aromatics sit above powerful tannins and rich fruit

Notes: Aglianico is an underrated variety and can offer wines of considerable ageworthiness and complexity. Like Nebbiolo's and Sangiovese's, Aglianico's tannins are felt on the gums and are almost always high and sandy-textured. Some points of difference are that alcohol here is generally lower than Nebbiolo, often at – or even below – 14%, and Aglianico is usually more deeply coloured than Sangiovese or Nebbiolo. As it comes from further south, Aglianico shows more mid-palate concentration; there is more flesh (fruit) than bones (tannins) here, while Nebbiolo can be the reverse.

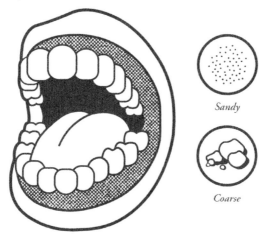

Sandy

Coarse

Perhaps the variety's most distinctive attribute is its complex, funky aromatic profile. It tends to be more unusual even than Nebbiolo's tar and roses; in Aglianico, look out for a particularly high-toned nose with savoury meaty, herbal and incense notes.

Confusions: See above for comments on Sangiovese and Nebbiolo. Aglianico has a darker, more earthy profile than Nerello Mascalese. Xinomavro is a reasonable confusion, but Aglianico is more savoury when compared to Xionmavro's more sweet-tasting fruit.

Producers: Mastroberadino, Feudi di San Gregorio, Molettieri (Taurasi); Grifalco, Elena Fucci (Vulture).

Nero d'Avola

Location of tannin: gums, rear gums

Type of tannin: grainy, sandy

Level of tannin: moderate

Construction: savoury acidity, tannins and a dry finish balanced by ripe fruit

Notes: Nero d'Avola has a medium to deep colour, moderate to high levels of grainy, sandy tannins felt on the gums (especially the rear gums) and moderate to high acidity. The fruit is ripe, occasionally rich and syrupy, with ample mid-palate concentration. Nero is relatively aromatic, with strong herbal and even meaty or tarry aromas and a dry finish. Nero is another example (along with Mourvèdre and Douro wines) of the 'ripe but dry' character of some southern European reds. Note that alcohol can be as low as 13%.

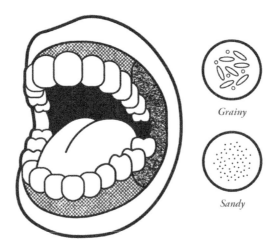

Grainy

Sandy

Nero d'Avola is the lesser of the two major Sicilian red varieties, occasionally rustic and rarely showing the complexity or beauty of Nerello Mascalese. Nonetheless, it is an important variety for the region and can add colour and body to a blend. This is yet another typically Italian variety in its focus on texture, tannins and acidity.

Confusions: The most obvious confusion for Nero d'Avola may be Aglianico, thanks to the herbal perfume, but expect greater finesse and elegance in Aglianico (and also in Nerello Mascalese). Nero is not as dense or dark coloured as Negroamaro but could be confused with Primitivo; the difference is simply that Nero has greater aromatic emphasis.

Producers: Feudo Marino, Cusumano, Caruso & Minini, Donnafugata (Sicily).

Nerello Mascalese

Location of tannin: gums

Type of tannin: sandy, grainy

Level of tannin: high

Construction: lifted aromas and delicate fruit contrast with powerful tannins

Notes: Sicily's Nerello Mascalese is one of Italy's great varieties but still remains unknown to many. It behaves like Nebbiolo in having moderate to high levels of tannins and alcohol (it can reach 14.5%) but somehow all within a body that feels light. The fruit is red, ripe and sweet tasting, but this is a wine whose focus is not fruit, but structure and texture: sandy or grainy tannins contrasting with silky fruit. Nerello Mascalese has a notably pale colour, with delicate, haunting aromas.

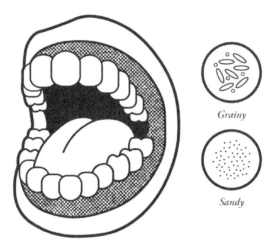

Grainy

Sandy

Confusions: Confusions for Nerello include Nebbiolo, but Nerello's mid-palate fruit is sweeter and more generous, and its aromas more simply red-fruited and floral rather than showing Nebbiolo's range of sweet and savoury. Aglianico is earthier and has a more funky, herbal aromatic spectrum. Other pale-coloured varieties such as Pinot Noir or Grenache lack Nerello's acid and tannin.

Producers: Graci, Passopisciaro, Planeta, Donnafugata, Tasca d'Almerita (Sicily).

Primitivo

Location of tannin: gums

Type of tannin: chalky

Level of tannin: moderate

Construction: firm, chalky tannins frame generous southern fruit

Notes: Primitivo (originally Croatia's Tribidrag) is a soft, sweet tasting, ripe, full bodied wine with firm, chalky tannins. The tannins are felt on the gums (Primitivo often shows much more rigid tannin structure than its American twin, Zinfandel). Primitivo is one of Italy's more internationally appealing grapes – juicy, dark fruited and concentrated, with ample mid-palate fruit. It can be raisiny; acidity is only moderate.

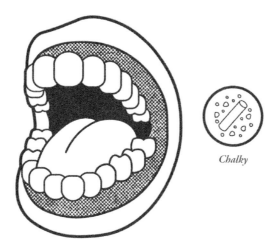

Chalky

Primitivo is often only mid ruby in colour and has a distinctive bitter tar/liquorice/herbal/almond note that Zinfandel rarely shows – a good example of how European wines from warm climates manage to preserve dry, savoury notes despite abundant ripe fruit.

Confusions: Primitivo is more structured and savoury than Zinfandel. It is softer and more easy drinking than the more funky, austere Negroamaro. It has softer, more generous fruit than Nero d'Avola.

Producers: Fatalone, Masseria Altemura, Masseria Cuturi, A Mano (Puglia).

Negroamaro

Location of tannin: gums

Type of tannin: coarse, grippy

Level of tannin: high

Construction: powerful tannins, a full body and ripe fruit make an intense wine

Notes: This is a more classically 'Italian' variety than southern neighbour Primitivo. In spite of its name, 'black bitter,' many examples are neither (although if you find both characteristics together, Negroamaro is a good bet, and some classic examples actually taste like *amaro,* the Italian liqueur).

Negroamaro should show: high levels of rustic, even coarse tannins (felt on the gums) and, if there is bitterness, it will be found on the grippy finish. Mid-palate fruit is limited, but what exists is soft and sweet-tasting, with a gamey, herbal, spicy, tarry edge. Acidity is moderate and, despite the tannins, Negroamaro can be a sweeter-tasting variety than Primitivo.

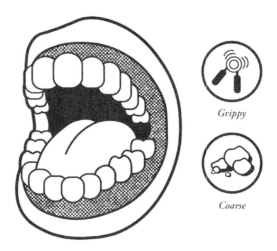

Grippy

Coarse

Confusions: Negroamaro is more rustic and less polished than Primitivo or Aglianico. It shows more body and tannin than Nero d'Avola.

Producers: Mocavero, Leone de Castris, Due Palme, Cantele (Puglia).

Other Wine Styles

The sections below are organised by wine style rather than by variety or geography. They cover the most important sparkling, sweet, fortified, rosé and orange wines commonly seen on international markets, with no offence to the many styles not mentioned.

Sparkling Wine

The keys to assessing sparkling wine are twofold: 1) identify the method of production used; and 2) assess the climate that could have given rise to the wine. Let us quickly look at the principal taste characteristics of the different methods of production.

Traditional method: wines which undergo their second fermentation in bottle tend to show: delicate, persistent strands of non-aggressive bubbles, some autolytic character (brioche, bready, yeasty flavours) and a balance between subtle fruit and more savoury notes.

Tank/charmat method: tends to create frothy, occasionally aggressive, loose bubbles; abundant, primary fruitiness and an absence of autolytic notes.

Traditional method wines

Champagne

Champagne is now produced in so many styles, it is increasingly hard to generalise about it. But all Champagne should show: a filigree acidity, a delicate but expressive fruit character and an overall cool climate sense of balance, precision and purity.

Identifying the varieties present in sparkling wine is one of the hardest tasks in blind tasting, but here are some general thoughts for the three major Champagne varieties.

Pinot Noir: Pinot Noir offers structure, power and body, with mid-palate concentration and focused fruit. It tends to be red-fruited with a golden colour in Blanc de Noirs examples.

Chardonnay: Chardonnay supplies a laser-like, linear acid structure, a lithe body and an overall finesse. It is less broad-shouldered than Pinot Noir; instead, more delicate and nervy. It is valuable for helping Champagne age gracefully.

Meunier: (no longer called Pinot Meunier in Champagne) offers loose-knit, soft mid-palate fruitiness and moderate acidity, without the firm structure of Pinot Noir. Thanks to its fruity generosity, it can appear more sophisticated than it really is; Meunier wines tend to drink well when young.

Stylistic differences in Champagne

Grande marque Champagne tends to exhibit a different character to the so-called 'grower Champagne' (small producer) style. Grande marque wines are often characterised by strong autolytic notes, can be quite reductive and often use full malolactic fermentation. Grower styles, meanwhile, show frequent use of oak, limited autolytic or malolactic fermentation notes, and an emphasis on purity of fruit and varietal expression. They can be quite 'naked' in displaying the characteristics of a vineyard, village, vintage or variety – a purity difficult to achieve for bigger houses constructing blends from across the region.

In general, non-vintage wines show more autolytic notes (perhaps due to the blending of various wines of different ages), while vintage wines are more purely-fruited. But the best method for identifying whether a wine is vintage or non-vintage is by assessing the finish: NV wines often finish on acid, while the more concentrated vintage wines finish on fruit.

Producers: Louis Roederer, Charles Heidsieck, Drappier (grande marques); Bérêche, Vilmart, Lallement, Chartogne-Taillet, Rodez, Savart, Jean Milan (growers).

English sparkling wine

The most consistent trait of English sparkling wines (ESW) is their elevated, steely acidity. This really can be searing in some examples, and in others, just very high. The acidity can have a green (malic acid) quality to it, as if the acidity itself is not quite ripe, and can also be felt separately from the fruit, rather than integrated into it (see Sauvignon Blanc).

Given their northerly origins, ESWs tend to exhibit less fruit than Champagne, so sometimes winemakers compensate with abundant autolytic notes or higher dosage. ESW is a classic example of traditional method winemaking, with delicate bubbles and precise flavours. Many extremely good examples of ESW now exist: do not underestimate them! **Producers:** Nyetimber, Coates and Seely, Chapel Down, Gusbourne, Ridgeview, Wiston.

Franciacorta

Along with English sparkling wine, Franciacorta is the closest lookalike to Champagne. It is the opposite of ESW in terms of ripeness, however: where ESW can struggle for fruit ripeness, Franciacorta's hallmark is ripe mid-palate fruit, correct for its southern origin. It is simply riper than ESW or Champagne.

Franciacorta can show considerable complexity, with high quality autolytic notes, and high – even racy – well integrated acidity (particularly in Blanc de Blancs examples). It can also show a distinctive waxy note. **Producers:** Ca' del Bosco, Bellavista, Majolini, Mosnel.

Crémants from France

Crémant d'Alsace: Pinot Blanc and Auxerrois are the main varieties. Look for high acidity paired with a soft, fruity mid palate. Here the Alsace varieties play the role of Meunier in Champagne: providing generous fruitiness. Another flattering aspect of the wine is its intense aromatic profile. All of this may lead you to thinking it is a better wine than it really is – but let it warm in the glass, and it will show a soft, oily texture typical of its region but not ideal for top quality sparkling wine. There are few autolytic notes in Crémant d'Alsace. **Producers:** Cattin, Dopff & Irion, René Muré.

Crémant de Loire: a number of varieties are permitted here, but chief among them is Chenin Blanc. Look out for the crescendo Chenin acid structure (see Chenin Blanc) with a particularly bracing acidity felt on the finish. In common with Crémant d'Alsace, Loire sparkling wines place little emphasis on autolytic notes. The usual Chenin Blanc aromatic salty funkiness should be in evidence. **Producers:** Langlois-Chateau, Bouvet-Ladubay, Gratien & Meyer.

Crémant de Bourgogne: made from Chardonnay and Pinot Noir, this is the closest lookalike to Champagne among the crémants. But the more southern origin gives more concentrated and riper mid-palate fruit, slightly less prominent acidity and less complexity and length. Of all the crémants, it has the most notable autolytic flavours and can show prominent red fruits. It usually lacks the tension and precision of Champagne, but its frothy fruitiness render it an enjoyable wine. **Producers:** Bailly-Lapierre, Simmonet-Febvre, Albert Bichot.

Crémant de Limoux: this should not be confused with Blanquette de Limoux, which (as the name suggests) is made predominantly from Blanquette (Mauzac). That wine shows intensely bruised apple fruit and very high acidity. Crémant de Limoux, meanwhile, is largely made from Chardonnay and Chenin Blanc (with a touch of Mauzac). This combination gives a powerful, linear acidity and, given its origins, riper fruit expression than the crémants of further north in France. In addition to its powerful acid structure, a defining feature of Limoux is its funky, earthy aromas. **Producers:** Sieurs d'Arques Toques et Clochers, Rives Blanques, Gérard Bertrand.

Cava

I am using the term Cava as a catch-all for northern Spanish sparkling wines made from the Cava varieties, even though some producers prefer not to use the appellation. Most notably, as of 2019, the Corpinnat designation requires its producers to source their fruit from the heart of the Penedès region, and this, along with other viticulture and winemaking requirements, is intended to elevate the quality of the wines. The Cava DO, likewise, has recently introduced new categories for longer aged wines.

Well-made Cava combines a Mediterranean ripeness of fruit with moderate acidity and creamy autolytic expression. Stone fruit flavours and measured (non-aggressive) acidity immediately render Cava a riper style than most European traditional method sparkling wines. Another point of distinction is the earthy, savoury, vegetal quality from the Xarello variety. The best Cavas, after many years on the lees, can show considerable complexity and depth and are one of the categories of sparkling wine improving most rapidly.

Inexpensive Cava can be rather characterless and have a high dosage (around 15g/l). These wines see only minimal time on the lees before disgorgement, so the bubbles have less finesse than Champagne or Franciacorta. In spite of the ripeness, Cava finishes dry and a touch earthy rather than on fruit. **Producers:** Gramona, Recaredo, Raventós i Blanc, Juvé y Camps, Cordorníu.

Sekt

Most German and Austrian Sekt is tank fermented, but better examples undergo secondary fermentation in bottle and are made from Riesling. Often bottle-fermented wines can show strong varietal aromas, with very high levels of acidity and limited autolytic character. **Producers**: Peter Lauer, von Schubert, Reichsrat von Buhl, Dr. Loosen (Germany); Bründlmayer (Austria).

Traditional method sparkling wines from outside Europe

These wines are produced in virtually every winemaking country, making it hard to generalise about them. The best way of approaching this category is to consider the ripeness of fruit as a guide to the climate that could have given rise to the wine.

Additionally, the notes below (see Tasting for Region of Origin) about winemaking styles by country are relevant: expect, for example, to see more evident winemaking notes such as autolysis in American sparkling wines than, say, in those of New Zealand. But all new world wines should show greater emphasis on fruit expression than those in Europe, which sometimes rely on autolysis, given their more limited fruit ripeness.

Other sparkling wines

Prosecco: Prosecco should be the most identifiable of all sparkling wines, thanks to its overt fruitiness. Prosecco is an aromatic wine, with abundant fruity aromas (particularly pear drop). It shows more aggressive, frothy and less persistent bubbles than traditional method styles. It lacks autolytic notes and shows less complexity and elegance than traditional method wines. Dosage is usually much higher than most realise – often 15g/l or more for high volume styles, and the alcohol is only 11% (although drier examples will see a concomitant rise in alcohol level to 12%). **Producers:** Mongarda, Ruggeri, Bisol, Nino Franco.

Moscato d'Asti: is identifiable by its grapey nose, frothy bubbles, very low alcohol and high levels of residual sugar. One important task with these wines is to distinguish between Moscato d'Asti and Asti (previously known as Asti Spumante). What are the differences? Moscato is much sweeter (around 115g/l compared to Asti's 80g/l), and Moscato shows lower alcohol (usually around 5.5% as opposed to 7.5% for Asti). Asti also has three bars of pressure compared to Moscato's two bars. **Producers:** GD Vajra, Vietti, Marcarini, Rizzi, Saracco.

Lambrusco: this should always be a very identifiable wine: fizzy, red (actually deep ruby) and usually slightly off dry. Although there are a number of different varieties of the Lambrusco grape (and DOCs!), expect a meaty/charcuterie nose, plenty of acidity, sour dark fruit profile, perceptible tannins (especially with the Salamino and Grasparossa varieties), an herbal twang and a distinct earthiness, offset by the frothy bubbles and residual sugar. Australian sparkling Shiraz is far more purely fruited, richer in fruit and body and has higher alcohol. **Producers:** Cleto Chiarli, Paltrinieri, Cavicchiolo, Moretto.

Sweet Wine

Assessing sweet wines requires knowledge of the analytical information concerning each wine type – i.e., what the sugar levels and alcohol levels should be. Please refer to Appendix III for this information. With this analytical data alone, you should never confuse, for example, German Auslese (90g/l residual sugar) with Sauternes (125g/l+ RS), and when you combine this with knowledge of what dry examples of the variety or region taste like, you will be a long way towards a correct identification.

Assessing sugar levels correctly is essential for accurate blind tasting identifications. My method is to take a classic example I am confident of and benchmark all other wines against it. For me, the benchmark is port. Port is always around 100g/l RS. So the question is: does this wine have more or less sugar than port? If it has more, it is a richer style (e.g. Sauternes, Tokaji, etc) and I can eliminate drier styles (most Vouvray, German Prädikats, etc). It is a quick way of narrowing the options.

A note on botrytis: many of the world's great sweet wines are made with the influence of botrytis. Being able to identify it makes your task as a taster a lot easier. So how to detect it? Botrytis is usually identified on the nose. It is one of the wine world's hardest aromas to pin down, but descriptions I have heard include: saffron, herbal tea, a slight chemical/plastic aroma. For me, it also has a kind of transparent quality: it is like looking at the fruit through a sheen. You are seeing (smelling) the fruit very clearly, but there is a layer between you and it.

One final point: sweet wines from Europe tend to finish with a dry or savoury note, just as European dry wines usually do. One of the most rewarding tensions of European sweet wines (fortified and non-fortified) is this interplay of sweet and savoury. Non-European sweet wines, meanwhile, more often tend to taste fully sweet throughout.

Sauternes

Sauternes is an outstanding – but not subtle – wine. It is emphatic in every way: full bodied, high alcohol (up to 14%), lusciously sweet, often 100% new French oak aged and stacked with tropical fruits and overt botrytis aromas.

It is noteworthy that nearby Barsac (its own appellation, though wines from Barsac are also entitled to use the Sauternes appellation) has a slightly more restrained style: citrus rather than tropical fruits, and with a savoury aroma that I often liken to onion skin. The acid is perkier in Barsac, and although analytically sugar levels may be the same as Sauternes proper, the wines feel lighter and brighter. **Producers:** Suduiraut, Guiraud, Tour Blanche (Sauternes); Doisy-Védrines, Coutet (Barsac).

Other French sweet wines

For Loire and Alsace sweet wines, please refer to the relevant sections on grape varieties. These examples do not tend to be much different stylistically to the dry styles, apart from the differences in alcohol and sugar. Simply learn the analytical information, know the dry versions by taste, and you will reach sensible conclusions.

German sweet wines

The analytical information again is the most important tool for identifying wines along the Prädikat scale; learn the standard sugar and alcohol levels, and you can make a sensible guess. But a few points to note: Kabinett and Spätlese usually are not made with botrytised berries. There may be more in Auslese, but really, these grapes are just riper berries with higher sugar content. BA and TBA wines are botrytised. And note that the frozen grapes for Eiswein do not usually have botrytis – they are just frozen! **Producers**: please refer to the recommendations under Riesling from Germany.

Austrian sweet wines

These wines tend to have Sauternes levels of sugar (but much lower alcohol), riper fruit than Germany, and often quite distinctive and diverse aromas, thanks to a whole range of different varieties used. Because of their diversity, they are difficult to identify blind. **Producers:** Alois Kracher, Heidi Schröck (Burgenland).

Tokaji

Tokaji should be an easy wine to identify, but simple lack of familiarity with it often stumps tasters. Five puttonyos wines (the most commonly seen of the fully sweet styles) start at around 150g/l RS, so they are intensely sweet. The alcohol is also notably low (11%). But Tokaji's strongest characteristic is its searing acidity, which feels as if it is among the highest of any white wines. Tokaji has a distinctive orange marmalade flavour to it. **Producers:** Royal Tokaji, Dereszla, Oremus, Disznókő.

Vin Santo

Italian Vin Santo is a difficult wine to identify. Made from a range of varieties, with extended ageing (without topping up), an amber colour, and with high alcohol but no fortification (often 15%+) and a range of sweetness (anywhere from 70-200g/l), it often tastes somewhat of acetaldehyde (like Fino or Manzanilla sherry).

A natural confusion might be a fortified style such as Madeira or Sherry, but Vin Santo has more fruit than either. It has fresh, concentrated fruit flavours when you get beyond the funky (occasionally volatile) aromas, and those from Tuscany can be very almondy. **Producers:** Felsina, Isole e Olena, Avignonesi, San Giusto a Rentennano.

Passito wines

Passito wines elsewhere in Italy tend to fall into traditional or fruit-led styles. Classic Recioto della Valpolicella, for example, can be very volatile, gamey and earthy with strong raisiny notes from the dried grapes. But more modern styles show more purity of fruit and are simply sweet versions of the dry wines of the region (Recioto di Soave would be a good example). **Producers:** Bertani, Masi, Allegrini (Valpolicella); Gini (Soave).

Botrytis styles from the new world

Look out for typical non-European purity of fruit, exaggerated by the botrytis. Some new world botrytised wines can veer towards being simply fruity and sweet (sometimes cloying) rather than showing any greater complexity.

Producers: de Bortoli Noble One (Riverina, Australia); elsewhere look for occasional bottlings from New Zealand, Australia, South Africa and USA with 'botrytis' plus the name of the grape variety, such as Riesling, Semillon or Sauvignon Blanc.

Ice wine

From Canada or Germany, ice wine has excellent purity of fruit, thanks to the absence of botrytis. The quality of the fruit is probably what gives away the identity of the wine most clearly: the fruit has a crystalline, jewel-like quality to it. The flavours have – literally – been crystallised into place through the harvesting and winemaking process. Varietal expression in ice wine is usually very transparent.

The Vidal variety is common in Canada and shows a musky aroma, with far less fruitiness than other ice wine varieties such as Riesling. **Producers:** Robert Weil (Rheingau); Dr. Loosen (Mosel); Dönnhoff (Nahe); Inniskillin (Niagara Peninsula, Canada).

Fortified Wine

The first and most important clue that you are tasting a fortified wine is the alcohol content. All fortified wine will show some heat on the finish, from just a little (15% Fino or Manzanilla) to a lot (port at 20%). Higher quality or longer-aged examples usually integrate the alcohol more successfully than inexpensive examples, where the alcohol can feel fiery on the finish.

Port

The different styles of port each have strong identities, but that does not mean they cannot be confused with other wines. Ruby, reserve and other inexpensive ports tend to be fiery, with rather unintegrated alcohol. Late Bottled Vintage wines have almost as much concentration of fruit as vintage wines but less complexity and tannin, as well as more suppleness and accessibility at a young age.

Tawny and colheita are much paler (more tawny!) in colour and show increasing oxidative notes with age. 10-year-old tawnies are still fruit-driven wines. 20-year-old wines have some nutty elements amid the fruit, while 40-year-old wines tend to be almost exclusively nutty. The longer the ageing, the more the alcohol integrates into the wine (this is also true of vintage styles).

Vintage port has changed in style considerably in the past decade or so, so it is worth revisiting this rather standard issue fine wine. The main point of difference in recent vintages, starting with 2011, is the handling of the tannin. No longer do you find any dry, abrasive tannins that take years to resolve. Recent vintages show ripe, fruity tannins. While certainly powerful, they are so enrobed by fruit that they are quite unobtrusive and render the wine thoroughly pleasurable from the time it is released in bottle.

One often overlooked aspect of all ports is that they are fortified by grape spirit at 'only' 77% abv, meaning the spirit retains some of its brandy flavour notes. So if you taste something that is reminiscent of Cognac or Armagnac, the wine is likely to be port. Madeira, Sherry and the Vins Doux Naturels are fortified with grape spirit at 96% abv (almost neutral spirit), so they lack the smoky, woody character of brandy.

Producers: Quinta do Noval, Taylor's, Warre's, Dow's, Fonseca (for LBV and vintage styles); Niepoort, Ramos Pinto, Graham's (for tawny styles).

Sherry

Perhaps the most important lesson about sherry is one about acidity. Or, it would be better to say, the lack of acidity. Tasters share an instinctive notion that there is plenty of acidity in sherry, perhaps because of the salty tang in Fino and Manzanilla. The truth is that in this baking climate for white grapes, acidity in sherry is medium at most. (Although with the significant qualification that sherry is often acidified).

The perception of acidity or vibrancy in the wine can often come from the phenolic grip in the oxidatively-aged wines, and the acetaldehyde of the biologically aged wines. Once this is understood, there should be no confusion with Madeira, which almost always has screamingly high levels of acidity (at least from the white grapes; Tinta Negra Mole has less).

Fino and Manzanilla: because they are biologically aged (under flor), the principal flavour characteristic of these wines is acetaldehyde (the nutty/salty/appley aroma). And since fortification is only to 15%, and the wines have been aged for years before release, the alcohol is often well integrated and seems lower than it really is. Manzanilla can be more saline than Fino.

Amontillado and Palo Cortado: these are very difficult to tell apart, as both feature biological (salty) and oxidative (nutty) ageing notes, and both usually show similar alcohol levels (around 17.5%). These wines can be very dry, especially if they are examples which have undergone extended ageing, enhancing the umami flavours and phenolic bitterness. They can have a 'hard' palate: no soft fruitiness here! Amontillado is an elegant, linear and lean wine rather than a heavy one. Palo Cortado can show Amontillado's linearity, but with the more savoury characteristics of Oloroso.

Oloroso: a bigger wine all around than the previous categories: full bodied, with higher alcohol (up to 20%) and greater levels of umami savouriness. Oloroso tends to be darker in colour than Amontillado and also shows a 'darker' nutty character — walnuts rather than hazelnuts. The longest-aged examples show so much savoury quality that they can be almost bitter on the finish.

Cream sherry: this remains a popular commercial style on the international market. Cream sherry is made from a base of Oloroso, sweetened with Pedro Ximinez (PX) to 130g/l, and is pale mahogany in colour. The aromas are those of the PX. Pale cream is lighter since the base is Fino, and shows sugar levels anywhere from 45-115g/l. **Pedro Ximinez** varietal bottlings show abundant raisin notes and a treacle-like texture (a concentration derived from the grape drying process).

Producers: Lustau, Hidalgo La Gitana, Barbadillo, González Byass, Valdespino, Equipo Navazos.

Madeira

The dominant feature of Madeira is *acidity*. There are various sweetness and alcohol levels (these are standardised across producers, so learn them for the different varietal styles: Verdelho, Sercial, Bual and Malmsey), but the acidity is the constant. It is what makes Madeira such a vibrant and never heavy wine. Once the acidity has led you to Madeira, all you have to do is assess the quality and the residual sugar level to arrive at a sensible guess.

The best Madeira are the varietally named wines. These have undergone significant oxidative ageing, so show considerable nutty oxidative aromas. But note that more entry-level wines like Rainwater and those made from the red variety Tinta Negra Mole can show far fewer oxidative notes (thanks to shorter ageing), as well as lower acidity and residual sugar than the varietal wines. In other words, while still being recognisably Madeira, they have reduced expressions of the key elements that make Madeira the wine it is.

Possible confusions for Madeira include tawny port, since it is far less easy than you might imagine to detect after long ageing whether a wine is made from white or red grapes. But Madeira is always a more linear, smoky wine than tawny, which is broader. Tawny also lacks the toasted, burned, toffee notes from the warm ageing process of Madeira.

Vin Santo is another possible confusion for entry level Madeira, showing almond notes, high alcohol and acidity. But the key difference is that Vin Santo is built on fruit while simple Madeira is built on sugar. Finally, oxidative sherry styles can be confusions, but the difference in acidity levels should set you straight. Also, sherry is only rarely sweet – for example, cream sherries – so sweetness is your first pointer towards Madeira, to be confirmed by the acidity. Some tasters have also noted a green tinge in the glass with Madeira.

Producers: Blandy's, Henriques & Henriques, Barbeito, d'Oliveiras.

Vins Doux Naturels

The Vins Doux Naturels (VDNs) from the south of France are an important wine style, even if only rarely seen on the international market. The best known is also the easiest to identify: Muscat de Beaumes de Venise. The high alcohol (15%) and the classic Muscat, grapey aromas make it a distinctive wine. The red VDNs can be more tricky to identify.

Maury and Banyuls, both made largely from Grenache, are the two most important red VDNs. They usually show alcohol of around 16.5%, with 90g/l RS. In other words, they are very similar analytically to Port. The alcohol is slightly lower, but when alcohol exceeds 15%, it can be difficult to distinguish between 16.5% and 20%.

Of the two, Banyuls shows more finesse and complexity, while Maury is more tannic (although bear in mind these are still Grenache tannins, so less structured than many tannins). But beyond the difference in alcohol levels, how do you distinguish either from a vintage or LBV port? The key here is the difference in the fortifying spirit.

As previously discussed (see Port), port shows some brandy, grapey notes thanks to the grape spirit used. But the aim of the VDNs is to showcase purity of fruit. For that reason, winemakers of VDNs use neutral spirit for fortification. So if the fruit flavours are particularly pure and expressive, you should consider a VDN before port.

Producers: Durban, Fenouillet, Bernardins, Vidal-Fleury (Muscat de Beaumes de Venise); Vignerons de Maury, Mas Amiel (Maury); Pietri-Geraud, Domaine de la Rectorie, Mas Blanc (Banyuls).

Rutherglen Muscat

Maybe the new world's most historical fortified wine style still in existence, Rutherglen Muscat should be easy to identify: the intense, sticky sweetness and the treacle, toffee, raisiny flavours are unlike anything else apart from Pedro

Ximinez (PX). The difference between the two is that, thanks to its hot, oxidative ageing, Rutherglen Muscat has a baked, roasted profile that PX lacks. PX instead shows a dried-fruit character.

Producers: Chambers Rosewood, Campbells, Buller.

Rosé Wine

Given the rise and rise of rosé, it is important to understand the characteristics of the major and classic rosé producing regions. For regions not listed, a combination of varietal and regional characteristics should be combined to arrive at a sensible guess.

Provence

The classic dry rosé is from Provence, where firm acidity, a silky texture, moderate alcohol and, above all, a refreshingly dry finish make for an eminently drinkable style. The finish is probably the biggest giveaway, finishing neither on fruit nor on acidity, but on dryness. Some Provence rosés also show an herbal edge, especially when made from the Rolle variety (Vermentino). **Producers:** d'Esclans, Miraval, Ott, Triennes, Peyrassol.

Bandol

Mourvèdre-based Bandol rosé is simply a bigger wine all around than the Grenache/Rolle wines from elsewhere in Provence. It shows a firm, broad-shouldered tannin structure and a strong herbal note with a dry finish. It is clearly an ageworthy wine, and the current vintage rarely shows as well as wines 1-2 years older. Bandol rosés are usually darker in colour than other Provence styles. **Producers:** Tempier, Pradeaux, Terrebrune, Pibarnon.

Tavel

Tavel is one of the deepest-coloured rosés, very sweet tasting (from the Grenache) and occasionally shows candied fruit. Tavel often displays structure, so it is easier to confuse with Bandol than with other Provence rosé, but Bandol is drier and probably more interesting. In common with other southern rosés, Tavel can show an herbal twang. **Producers:** Aquéria, Mordorée, Guigal, Prieuré de Montézargues.

Sancerre

Sancerre rosé is made from Pinot Noir, with the attendant aromas, silky texture, delicate red fruits and fine acidity. This is usually a pale-coloured rosé. **Producers:** André Dezat, Gerard Boulay, Henri Bourgeois, Alphonse Mellot.

Marsannay

Marsannay is the most important village for rosé from Burgundy. The wines are distinctly Pinot Noir with all the finesse that entails but show more structure and body than their Sancerre equivalents, and they certainly have the capacity for one or more years ageing after bottling. Good Marsannay rosé tastes like fine, delicate, red Burgundy, with a hint of earthiness. **Producers:** Audoin, Pataille, Bruno Clair, Roty.

Spanish rosado

The biggest production area for Spanish rosado is Rioja, although most of us tend to think of Navarra as being the home of Spanish rosé. Navarra's Garnacha-based rosado is a juicy, fruity, red-fruited, riper wine than the drier French styles, and it has a deeper colour. Rioja rosado tends to be a little more restrained in terms of its fruit but still shows more ripeness than French examples. **Producers:** Ochoa, Chivite (Navarra); CVNE, Muga, Marqués de Riscal, Marqués de Cárceres (Rioja).

Italian rosato

These wines are produced from all over the country, making it difficult to generalise, but as always with Italian wines, look out for a marked acidity, a tart red-fruit character and an herbal accent. **Producers:** GD Vajra (Piedmont); Rocca di Montegrossi (Chianti); Graci (Sicily).

Orange Wines

Extended skin contact not only gives the deeper colour the name indicates, but more importantly gives a powerful sense of structure and phenolic grip. In a black glass, you might imagine that you are dealing with a mid-weight red wine with firm tannins. I find less purity of fruit expression in orange wines than in conventionally-made white wines. It is as if the phenolics extracted during skin contact 'smudge' the fruit flavours. The finish on orange wines is often quite long and grippy.

Producers: Jean-Yves Peron (Savoie, France); Herdade do Rocim (Alentejano, Portugal); Occhipinti (Sicily, Italy); Strohmeier (Styria, Austria); Dakishvili (Kakheti, Georgia); Maturana (Maule, Chile); Hermit Ram (Canterbury, New Zealand); and many others. Many producers now experiment with an orange wine in their range.

Tasting for Region of Origin

If you are tasting to identify a variety, the tips in the previous section should help. But if you are working to identify a region of origin, a different set of skills is necessary. Master these, add in your knowledge of varieties, and you should become a much more confident taster.

There are two aspects to tasting for origin, and I will deal with each in turn. First, in *general terms*, how is it possible to assess where a wine may have been grown/produced? And second, while I have already discussed wine styles specific to important regions, variety by variety, what can we say about general characteristics of major wine producing countries?

Tasting for Origin: General Considerations

These tips are designed to help you establish a general sense of the *kind of climate* a wine may have been grown in. They should be combined with the regionally specific tips detailed in the varieties sections in order to make a reliable guess at origin.

Fruit ripeness

This is the most obvious category. In general terms, the riper the fruit profile, the warmer the climate of origin is. Yes, there are numerous exceptions. But, in general, cooler regions in northern Europe produce wines with less ripe fruit than those around the Mediterranean. The cool Adelaide Hills region of Australia produces less fruit ripeness than the warm McLaren Vale.

How do you detect fruit ripeness? First, by the flavours of the fruit. In white wines, cooler climate wines will have little fruit beyond simple citrus or

172

green apple notes. Moderate climates might introduce orchard or stone fruit, while warmer climates will show tropical notes. In reds, the transition may be from light red fruits to black and blue fruits.

Second, you detect ripeness by the character of the fruit. In white wines, the transition from cool to warm is marked by a movement from restrained (even neutral) fruit character to one that is generously fruity and even opulent.

In red wines, the fruit character moves from tart, crisp and crunchy, to soft, smooth and even baked or raisined. Both simple Valpolicella and Châteauneuf-du-Pape may smell of strawberry, but in each, the strawberry assumes a very different character. In Valpolicella, it is light, tart and perhaps crunchy. In Châteauneuf, it is soft and even jammy.

Fruit flavours and the character of those flavours are good starting points for assessing climate of origin but need to be supplemented by other characteristics in order to ensure a logical identification.

Fruit density

Density of fruit is the weight of the fruit on the tongue: how light or heavy it is. In general terms, warmer climates are likely to give more dense fruit than cooler climates. Think of light northern French white wines: Muscadet, Chablis or Sancerre as opposed to the richer, more weighty whites of further south: Mâcon, Condrieu or Bordeaux.

Fruit density has a direct relationship to the ripeness of the grapes at harvest. This is the difference between a Pinot Noir from Germany and one from Sonoma; the riper Californian wine from a warmer climate will show much greater fruit weight on the palate.

Alcohol level

Alcohol level appears to be a relatively straightforward indicator for climate. The higher the alcohol, the warmer the climate. However, there are so many exceptions and complicating factors that one must never take this piece of evidence by itself. In very broad brushstrokes, though, warmer climates yield higher-alcohol levels.

The way to assess alcohol levels is twofold. First, think about the overall weight of the wine on the palate. Alcohol is a key contributor to weight. One of the reasons Mosel Kabinett is so light-bodied is because the alcohol is so low. While an Argentinian Malbec may have considerable density of fruit, the high alcohol also contributes to the sensation of weight on the palate.

The second way to assess alcohol level is the sense of heat or burning felt on the back of the throat after spitting/swallowing (you do not need to swallow to experience this). I only really experience any heat at all above 12% alcohol (that is why if it is a low alcohol wine under 12%, I have difficulty pinning down the precise alcohol). Above 12%, a gradually increasing sense of heat in the throat – which can become a burn in fortified wines – is an excellent means of arriving at an accurate assessment of alcohol level. Line up wines starting at 12% and increasing by 0.5% alcohol each time, and you will soon identify the level of heat you associate with each alcohol level (with the qualification that many stated alcohol levels on labels are far from accurate).

Body

The body of a wine overlaps with the discussion both of fruit density and of alcohol. Body is given by: fruit density, alcohol level, tannin level (in reds) and phenolic content (in whites) as well as winemaking choices such as lees ageing or use of oak. Often, but not always, warmer climates tend to be associated with increased levels of these factors, yielding fuller-bodied styles.

While not a totally reliable measure by itself (for instance, a Langhe Nebbiolo from a relatively warm climate may have 14% alcohol and still not be considered a full-bodied wine), a fuller body is usually associated with a warmer climate, and a lighter body with a cooler one. The easiest way to assess body weight is to ask: how mouth-filling is this wine? Fuller bodied wines fill the mouth; lighter bodied wines do not.

Acidity

Particularly pertinent to white wines, acidity can reveal a lot about a wine's origin. But rather than simply focus on the *level* of acidity, which is too dependent on the variety used (Riesling will always have high acidity, wherever it is grown – if it does not, it should be torn up!), I prefer also to think about how integrated the acidity is into the body of the wine.

In general, white wines from cooler climates have *less well integrated acidity* than whites from warmer climates. The acidity in a Muscadet or an entry level Alsatian Riesling really sticks out. But even a little further south, in northern Italy, the supposed 'high' acidity of Italian wines is far less obvious in examples like Gavi or Pinot Grigio, where the acidity is more 'tucked into' the body of the wine. The integration of the components is superior — although that does not make the wines superior to their northern rivals. Even in some red wines — especially lighter ones — you find the same syndrome: consider high altitude, moderate climate Chianti Classico compared to warmer Brunello di Montalcino. The acidity sticks out far more in the Chianti.

X factors

While all of the above elements will help you identify the type of climate a wine was grown in, there are so many exceptions that one must proceed with extreme caution. To name a few key ones:

Varietal characteristics: Chenin Blanc in relatively warm South Africa *should* give a moderate to full bodied wine with softer acidity. But no! The character of the variety speaks louder than the place, and the acidity remains very shrill.

You might expect Cabernet Sauvignon grown in warm western Australia to be ripe or even opulent, but Margaret River gives a medium bodied, leafy expression – a textbook example of the variety.

Altitude: grapes grown at altitude generally give lighter-bodied wines than their cousins in the valleys, and often a lifted aromatic quality.

Unexpected climates: Alsace may be in northern Europe (further north than Sancerre), but in the rain shadow of the Vosges Mountains and with many of its hillside sites acting as sun traps, the wines behave as if from a warmer climate: they are frequently full-bodied, opulent, ripe and soft.

Unusual wine styles: Hunter Valley Semillon has low alcohol and pronounced acidity but is grown in a warm-to-hot region. It is simply harvested very early. You have to learn these exceptions one by one.

Winemaking choices: particular ways of vinifying and ageing wines can obscure their origins. Carbonic maceration, for example, can make heavier red varieties from warm regions taste much lighter. That is one reason why winemakers may use the technique.

Stylistic Norms by Country

What follows is a discussion of wine style by country. That is, I argue that entire countries can show consistent traits in their wine styles, across regions, varieties and wine colour. Factors such as climate, winemaking choices and even tradition can influence wine style, country by country.

Before discussing each country, though, it is helpful to review the fundamental difference between European and non-European ('new world') wines. At the most basic level, European wines tend to be more savoury and dry than new world wines. European wines may have plenty of fruit, but fruit is rarely the focus of the wine. The best example of this is the finish, where even warmer-climate European wines from around the Mediterranean tend to finish dry. Additionally, they may contain earthy notes.

By contrast, non-European winemakers tend to place their emphasis on purity of fruit expression. Often these more fruit-focused wines will finish on fruit rather than finish very dry.

When it comes to white wines, winemakers from cool parts of northern Europe are often quite relaxed about leaving residual sugar in them. Due to the generally warmer climate of non-European growing regions, residual sugar is rarely seen in quality wines from outside Europe.

For red wines, non-European winemakers often make wines with riper, more supple tannins that allow even the biggest reds to be approachable upon release. European winemakers, by contrast, are less concerned with making their wines accessible when very young. Firm, even abrasive tannins are commonly found in young European wines.

France

French wines are hugely diverse: from the driest, purest Chablis in the north to the most opulent Châteauneuf-du-Pape in the south. But within this vast stylistic range, there are certain consistent markers that typify French wines.

Balance. This is not an easy characteristic to describe, but it drives right to the heart of what French winemaking is all about. Balance in wines is really a question of *drinkability* — when there is nothing that creates resistance to the wine being drunk; no single component sticks out as an obstacle for the drinker to overcome. French wines are rarely too acidic or too tannic. Usually the alcohol is well integrated, even among the ripest southern wines. Where there is generous fruit, it is balanced against a freshness of acidity and a dryness on the finish. French wines are almost never *excessive* in any one feature.

Dryness. French table wines are *dry*. This point cannot be emphasised too much. In both white and red wines, the fruit has a dry quality which leaves the palate clean and fresh rather than cloying. These are ideal food wines.

Winemaking. French winemaking tends to be relatively hands-off. That means that you rarely taste the intervention of the winemaker. This is not to say that techniques like new oak or bâtonnage are not used, just that they are usually well integrated and non-obtrusive.

Subtlety. French winemaking consistently aims for understatement rather than bombast; elegance rather than force. Of course there are many powerful wines in France, but good ones will always show subtlety and complexity – elements that often emerge with age.

Ageworthiness. While the bulk of French wine — like that of every other country — is made for immediate consumption, among the classic appellations, French wines are not only ageworthy but often made in such a way as to discourage premature drinking. Many classic wine regions unapologetically still make tight, tannic wines that need years in bottle to resolve.

Italy

Italy is the land of characterful reds made from indigenous varieties and palate-cleansing whites, some of which have considerable charm but many of which resemble each other. Nonetheless, a broad way of thinking about Italian wines is that this is the land of freshness and texture rather than of overt fruit expression. Of course there is plenty of fruit in Italian wines, but it is far from being the focus; learning to enjoy the pithy-textured whites and grainy reds is fundamental to appreciating Italian wines. The focus on acidity and texture means that Italy's wines come alive with food, developing considerably more charm and complexity than when tasted alone.

It is helpful to divide this country's large production into white and red wines. Both have distinctive Italian traits which can steer your country guesses.

White wines: Italy produces a sea of white wine made from local varieties. In general, these do not overflow with character. Nonetheless, it is possible to make a few general remarks. Italian whites show moderate to high levels of firm acidity, usually linear in shape. This linearity gives a sense of direction or purpose to the wines (see also Chardonnay, Pinot Gris). The acidity is well integrated into the body of the wine (more so than in wines made further north in Europe, probably thanks to Italy's warmer climate), meaning that it is rarely obtrusive.

Italian whites tend to exhibit phenolic grip, especially on the finish, thanks to the national convention of firm pressing of the fruit. This phenolic content adds some bite and interest to not always very expressive fruit. These are quintessentially back palate as opposed to front palate wines (I owe this point to Mary Gorman MW). What that means is that while they are not laden with fruit on entry (as many non-European wines are), their subtleties are revealed on the finish, where they can show a gentle perfume and often a nuttiness or subtle fruitiness. They are usually understated but elegant wines.

Red wines: almost all Italian reds are built on two things: acid and tannin. The high level of acidity present in virtually all Italian reds is a huge giveaway for the country, but also risks the production of volatile acidity, a relatively common component of many classic Italian reds, picked up on the nose as nail polish remover or balsamic vinegar. Italian tannins are frequently grainy, sandy or otherwise slightly abrasive, and in general they are far less polished than French tannins.

Fruit is not the focus' of Italian reds, which is why they so desperately cry out for food: even in those from warmer climates, the emphasis falls more squarely on tannin and acidity as dominant features of the wine. Many Italian reds show limited mid-palate concentration, and many are completely or close to monovarietal rather than being blends. That means that varietal expression tends to be pure and unobscured.

Wines from the north of the country will often show some angularity and precision compared to the roundness of southern wines. Tart red fruits (especially sour red cherry) and herbal nuances are common in all Italian reds.

In both white and red wines, winemaking is rarely obtrusive other than in more modern styles. With the exception of the Super Tuscans and other modern producers, the influence of new oak is limited; old or large oak is the norm. Do not expect to find a winemaker's fingerprints all over the wine. This is particularly true of Italian reds post-2011, a new era of winemaking in which purity of varietal and terroir expression is prized over power and density (a style that predominated from the mid 1990s until around 2010). We are happily living in a glorious era for Italian wine.

Spain

The small number of internationally available Spanish white grape varieties all have distinctive characteristics (see Tasting for Variety), making it hard to generalise about them. However, the whole gamut of Spanish red wines tends to be identifiable as originating from the same country.

Spain's climate, generally warmer than France's, gives rise to full-bodied, powerful reds. Wines from northwest Spain or Rioja may be exceptions, but wines that feature large amounts of Garnacha or Monastrell can be very powerful, sweet-tasting and even jammy. In wines that feature more Tempranillo, chalky tannins and firm acidity are common, coupled to a supple texture.

Spanish reds often show interventionist winemaking, in which the wine style is determined by work in the cellar. New oak is the most obvious example, including the use of American oak. In Rioja, oxidative ageing of wines is common in traditional styles.

Most Spanish reds are blends, so while varietal character can still be identified, they often lack the precision and purity of, say, Italian reds.

Germany

Increasing amounts of high quality, silky Pinot Noir (Spätburgunder), rich Chardonnay and layered Pinot Blanc are produced in Germany, but in general the international focus remains steadfastly on Riesling. For all varieties in Germany, look out for: high acidity; fragrant aromas; limited use of new oak other than in a few warmer, more southern regions; and a generally hands-off style of winemaking, with an emphasis on expressing purity of variety and place.

Austria

In general, Austria is notable for richly-textured, savoury whites which have not undergone malolactic fermentation. In wines of both colours are found a peppery flavour/texture and (associated with that pepperiness) a tangy, reverberant acidity.

United States

While all over the country there are many new, experimental producers who diverge from classic American winemaking styles, nonetheless some general statements can be made about most American wines. First, these are fruit-led wines. The US makes wines where fruit comes first, every time. Associated with that is America's technically very clean winemaking, with an emphasis on purity of fruit. Only Australia and New Zealand can match the faultlessly clean winemaking of the US. This is not the land of brett (see Wine Faults).

Ripeness is a hallmark of US wines. Many regions of California are *so ripe*; the generosity of fruit can be a giveaway; and the same applies to Washington state. Even allegedly cool climate Oregon, depending on specific site, can give full-bodied Pinot Noir and Chardonnay. New York and Virginia make more restrained styles, but (except for Finger Lakes Riesling), these wines remain obscure on the international stage.

Textural richness is another consistent characteristic of American wines. A combination of the emphasis on fruit and west coast ripeness often gives very richly textured wines that caress the palate in an almost hedonistic way. Finally, the US often produces wines that show the hand of the winemaker, whether through generous oak use, intense extraction, or use of stems for varieties like Pinot Noir and Syrah.

Australia

Australia produces almost every variety you can think of but nonetheless maintains some consistent stylistic attributes. First, fruit ripeness comes quite easily in Australia. This is not the country of hard tannins or tart whites from unripeness. Supple, ripe fruit is the norm. Second, like US winemakers, Australian producers favour technically clean winemaking with a focus on expressing purity and clarity of fruit flavours. Fruit clarity is used as the vehicle for expressing variety, climate and place.

Australia prizes varietal expression: velvety Shiraz, leafy Cabernet, petrolly Riesling — Australian winemakers do not attempt to change a variety's natural tendencies. This goes hand in hand with Australian winemakers' tendency to being hands-off: rarely do you detect overt winemaking techniques in the wines beyond very clean fruit.

Australia is producing increasingly balanced wines. Huge Barossa Shiraz styles that were popular in the first decade of this century are still available, but, increasingly, Australia is moving towards earlier picking, fresher and more balanced styles for both colours, particularly with Shiraz and Bordeaux varieties. For whites, early picking is common: low alcohol styles of Riesling, Semillon and Marsanne are classics — perhaps unexpectedly — from this warm climate.

New Zealand

Of all the new world countries, New Zealand shares the most climatic similarities with cooler parts of Europe. New Zealand makes mid-weight, balanced, moderate alcohol wines in both colours and all styles.

New Zealand completes the trinity of countries focused on clean, fruit-led styles, but the difference from the US or Australia is that the fruit here expresses itself in a crisp, cool climate register.

Whether due to their restrained ripeness levels, or their emphasis on fruit purity, rarely in these wines do you taste winemaking. While New Zealand's famed Sauvignon Blanc often uses selected yeasts to enhance aromas, it would be difficult to declare that with any confidence: that is what I mean when I say rarely do you *taste* winemaking. One exception may be reductive styles of Chardonnay (see 'reduction' in Wine Faults).

South Africa

This is another country changing before our eyes, with cooler southern regions and the now fashionable Swaartland producing styles a far cry from the old stereotypes of rustic, rubbery, smoky Pinotage or Cabernet Sauvignon. Many of these new styles are varietally expressive, fresh and balanced.

Probably the most identifiable aspect of South African wines is their 'one foot in Europe, one foot in the new world' character. That strange definition captures a lot of what South African wine is about, particularly with regard to the reds. What it means is that South Africa often shows the fruit ripeness, intensity, and body of a warm climate, non-European origin. But at the same time there is a savoury, dry quality reminiscent of Europe, particularly on the finish. These are far less obviously fruit-led wines than most new world wines and are among the new world's driest wines.

Chile

Chile produces the full range of international varieties, but, fortunately for tasters, it displays a number of signature characteristics, foremost among which is high acidity. Chile contains a multitude of climates and altitudes, but, for whatever reason, high acidity is a characteristic of both reds and whites throughout the country. This is particularly evident in the red wines, where Syrah and the Bordeaux varieties show noticeable acidity.

Although they can be made so, red wines are rarely of the blockbuster variety in Chile. Varieties that can be very powerful elsewhere — Syrah, Cabernet — are usually medium to full bodied here, and, with their electric acidity, feel vibrant rather than heavy.

The presence of herbaceous notes in both Chilean whites and reds has occasioned much comment by tasters, but perhaps overstated: there are many purely fruited Chilean wines. However, it is true that many Chilean wines show an herbaceous edge, particularly those made from varieties with high levels of pyrazines, such as the Bordeaux varieties. Other instances of greenness may simply be due to unripeness (e.g. from harvesting excessively high yields).

Argentina

For white wines, Argentina is defined by Torrontés and Chardonnay. Torrontés should be quite identifiable (see Torrontés). Chardonnay can be ripe and a touch generic. The reds, however, are more distinctive, with a trio of key features: tannins, power and dryness.

Argentina's principal challenge in its red wines is to manage the tannins. These can often be big and a touch rustic and can easily dominate the wine. With Cabernet Sauvignon or Malbec, Argentina gives concentrated, inky, full-bodied reds, although some producers are now working to produce more moderate styles, particularly from high altitude sites. Pinot Noir from Patagonia can be very light.

Argentina's reds are among the driest of any from the new world, with savoury finishes. The closest comparison may be with South Africa, but Argentinian reds tend to show more purity of fruit than South Africa's earthy reds do.

Other countries

I have only covered the most important producing countries on the international markets here, with no offence intended to those I have left out. In general, however, the countries I have omitted do not possess strong stylistic norms across different varieties and regions, so they are better approached on a variety rather than a country basis. Please see Tasting for Variety for tips on identifying varieties grown in those countries.

Tasting for Quality

Identifying wines blind is little better than a parlour game unless you can correctly assess the single most important aspect of any wine: *how good it is*. It is unfortunate how many tasters struggle with this aspect, the most important commercial skill for any wine professional. One of the main reasons for the difficulty is the absence of a systematic approach to assessing quality. I offer one here.

TBLICA

Master of Wine students use this mnemonic to assess quality. If all six of the lettered components are considered, an appropriate appraisal of quality should follow.

Typicity: this is a controversial component to start with. What makes a wine 'typical' of where it comes from/what variety it is? For our purposes, the answer is simple: it tastes like what previous or classic versions of this wine taste like.

This is an unsatisfactory answer for those who argue that, for example, grower Champagne is more authentic and typical of the region than the traditional grandes marques style. But in a professional setting, being able to benchmark a wine against classic examples is an important skill — if only because it gives you the option to choose a 'typical' example, or to know that you are choosing an 'atypical' one.

For the purposes of wine exams, typicity is considered a virtue. The more a wine resembles well-known expressions of the region or variety, the better it is considered to be. Again, there are many reasons to criticise this approach, but, for now, wine exams still reward recognising typicity, so we work on that basis. That is why it is important constantly to taste classic examples of worldwide wine styles in order to know what is typical – and then to use these as your benchmark. My hope is that the wines made by the producers I recommend in this book are 'classic examples' of their types.

Balance: a balanced wine is one that puts up no resistance to being drunk. It has no single component that 'sticks out,' causing the drinker to pause. It shows a seamless harmony of all the different elements of the wine; it is an integrated whole, greater than the sum of its parts.

An unbalanced wine shows one or more obstacles to drinkability, e.g., the tannins are abrasive; the acidity is not integrated; the alcohol burns. Any features which are not in harmony with the rest of the wine render the wine unbalanced.

When discussing balance, it is important to note that one component of the wine cannot be 'balanced.' It must be in balance with another element. E.g., 'high alcohol is balanced by fruit concentration;' 'residual sugar is balanced by acidity,' etc.

Length: this is one of the easiest elements to identify, but also one of the most underrated in terms of its importance. Length is simply how long the wine's flavours persist after you spit/swallow.

Entry-level wines will fade within seconds, while the world's best wines continue to be experienced for minutes afterwards. Note that you should continue to taste the fruit of the wine. Persistence of fruit is a sign of concentration and ageworthiness, and therefore of quality. If you are tasting just acid or tannin, the wine is less good.

Intensity of flavour: intensity of flavour is how strongly perceived the flavours of a wine are. High intensity means that the flavours are particularly focused and expressive. The greater the intensity of flavour, the better the wine. Wines with less flavour intensity will tend to show a shorter finish, while the best wines saturate the palate with flavour. Note that intensity of flavour is unrelated to body weight: even the lightest wines can have remarkable flavour intensity (think of Champagne or Mosel Riesling).

Concentration: concentration in a wine means concentration of fruit. Usually this is perceived on the tongue. Concentrated wines show very focused fruit on the mid palate, while less concentrated wines are more 'watery.' For watery, think of inexpensive, neutral whites at low prices. Concentration is unrelated to body weight. You can have a concentrated Muscadet just as easily as a concentrated Napa Cabernet.

Concentration is a virtue in wine because it gives depth to a wine, a longer finish and extends ageability. Wines lacking concentration are not destined for a long life.

Ageability: or ageworthiness, is a fundamental attribute of fine wine, and even modest wines can have ageing potential beyond immediate consumption. However, it is important to distinguish between wines that will 'hold' – i.e. maintain their current profile without improving; and those that will improve with age, as the tannins soften, oak flavours and acidity integrate, and the flavours develop greater complexity. Generally speaking, powerfully structured, concentrated wines with high intensity of flavour are likely to improve with age. Those with simple flavour profiles and lacking concentration will not.

Other important features

Complexity: a wine is complex when it shows multiple flavours simultaneously, rather than just one. That can mean a diversity of fruit/vegetable/floral flavours along with earthiness, minerality and oak notes. The most simple wines taste only of one fruit.

Beauty: this is a more subjective notion than any of the previous categories, but a vitally important one for the appreciation and understanding of wine. Beauty in wine usually requires most if not all of the categories above to be fulfilled. But even if these are all checked off, there can be an additional, more ephemeral quality present.

Beauty consists in a harmony of all the elements in a wine; an irresistible allure that eludes easy explanation, and a sense that the taster is in the presence of something unique and special. Beauty in wine is hard to describe, but easy to identify when it is found. For the greatest wines, it is the most important category of all, and encapsulates and brings to consummation all the others.

Miscellaneous Advice

Tasting Blends

Sometimes it can be helpful to establish whether a wine is made from a single variety or a blend of varieties. In general, blends show: a deeper colour (in red wines); less clarity and precision of flavour, but potentially more complexity (since there is more than one note sounding); and some sense that different ingredients are adding different elements to the wine. For example, in a Languedoc blend, the generous, sweet fruit may come from Grenache, but it feels unnatural that the acidity would. That does not mean the acidity does not harmonise, just that it may be contributed by a different variety.

By contrast, mono-varietal wines display purity and precision of flavour at the risk of showing what some might perceive as a 'defect' – e.g. sparse mid-palate concentration in Nebbiolo or Cabernet Sauvignon, or lack of acidity in 100% Grenache wines. But the winemaker (or convention!) has decided that the virtues of the single variety outweigh these supposed defects.

Wine Faults

Readers are referred to Jamie Goode's excellent book, *Flawless*, the indispensable guide on this subject which explains the causes of diverse wine faults. Below are a few comments to help tasters identify some common ones.

Brettanomyces: 'brett' in red wines has fans and detractors, but whether or not you consider it a fault, it is important to be able to recognise it. It has a particularly pungent aroma of sweaty horse and barnyard. These features may be confused with leathery development in an older red wine, but in brett-infected wines, they appear from the beginning of the wine's life. Brett-infected wines often taste metallic on the finish.

Brett is particularly prevalent in the Rhône Valley (north and south), Bordeaux, Loire Cabernet Franc and some traditional Italian wines. It is only rarely found in the new world, where clean winemaking is the order of the day.

Cork taint/TCA: the wine simply smells and tastes like cork, damp cardboard or something dank. The fruit is 'stripped.' Usually most evident on the nose and finish.

Geosmin: a very under-analysed fault. Geosmin is a form of intense earthiness which tastes like beets/beetroot (geosmin is found in that vegetable). While many European wines are earthy, geosmin-tainted wines smell of soil and mould, and the fruit expression is muted as a result.

Mousiness: an unknown wine fault until a few years ago, now common thanks to the rise of zero-sulphur wines. Mousiness cannot be detected on the nose, and only to a limited degree on the mid palate. But it dominates the finish, where a rancid taste of mouse droppings overwhelms the fruit flavours. It is most commonly found in wines bottled with limited or no added sulphur.

Oxidation: white wines take on a darker colour, and the fruit is 'maderised' – it tastes like Madeira (which is intentionally oxidised). That is, it is nutty rather than fresh and fruity. The same thing happens in red wines, where the flavours are pruney, raisiny and of dried rather than fresh fruit. Heat damage to a bottle can cause oxidised notes but often results in a wine stripped of all fruit.

Reduction: in over-simplified terms, reduction is the name given to the condition of a wine which has been exposed to very little oxygen; in this sense, it is the opposite of oxidation. Negative reduction shows as a smell of blocked drains, rotten eggs, onions or cabbage.

More positive reduction takes the form of the sulphurous 'struck match' aroma in white wines (enjoyed by some tasters), limited fruit expression, and an overall tightness and precision to the nose and palate.

Some red varieties, particularly Syrah and occasionally Pinot Noir, are more prone to reduction. This is usually expressed in the 'blocked drains' spectrum of aromas and muted fruit.

Volatile acidity: 'VA' is a fault that is often associated with Italian reds, which are prone to it thanks to their naturally high acidity and extended, oxidative oak ageing. Volatility in a wine is detected on the nose as the lifted aroma of vinegar or nail polish remover. Like many other wine faults, it can in limited quantities add interest and complexity. But it can also overwhelm a wine and overshadow the other flavours. Many old to very old oak-aged wines are affected by volatile acidity.

Appendix I:

How to Approach Blind Tasting Exam Questions

Variety questions

If the question is simply 'what is the variety?', focus first on the most noteworthy aspects of the wine. Is it particularly tannic, or acidic, or sweet? That will narrow your options immediately. Then use structure to narrow further, perhaps construction too, finally using flavour and colour as confirmatory evidence.

Origin questions

If the question is, 'where does this wine come from?', the first thing to ponder is, what kind of climate could have given rise to this wine? Is the fruit ripe and rich, or light and fresh? How dense is the fruit, and how high is the alcohol? (see Tasting for Region of Origin). When you have decided whether it comes from a cool, moderate or warm climate, consider the wine style. Does it show the emphasis on fruit typical of new world winemaking? Or is it more earthy, as many European wines are? Finally, use your knowledge of countries and regional specifics to arrive at a sensible conclusion.

Quality questions

Using the TBLICA template discussed in Tasting for Quality, assess the levels of each of those categories. Simple wines will show low levels of each.

Mid-level wines will show mostly moderate levels of each, and high quality wines will show mostly high levels. The very best wines, in addition to showing high levels of each, will show considerable complexity and beauty.

Vintage questions

If you are asked 'what vintage is this?', it is likely that the wine comes from one of the classic European wine regions or one of a few important non-European regions. This is simply because vintage is considered both to be particularly marked in these classic regions, and because the quality of a vintage can be so commercially important.

After identifying the region, the key to vintage assessment is to consider the ripeness and overall style of the wine. If a red wine is particularly generous and fruity, with ripe tannins, it could come from a warmer than usual vintage. Or if a white wine is tart and showing limited fruit, the vintage could have been difficult.

Particularly important is to consider the finish, which, even when there appears to be abundant fruit, will reveal how truly ripe the grapes were. If the wine finishes on acid rather than fruit, it is likely to be from a lesser vintage.

Please go to vintagevariation.com/vintages for my analysis of recent vintages in classic regions.

Wine style questions

As with all aspects of describing a wine, you need to have a vocabulary to hand to be able to describe its style. The best way I have heard wine style described is as the one line description on a wine's back label. At two extremes, examples might be: 'a fruity everyday wine' or 'a traditional, ageworthy red.'

In other words, style questions get to the heart of the wine: what is this wine's purpose? What is it *trying to be*? Rather than a rehash of the quality components, style is instead a more holistic appraisal of the character or personality of the wine.

Some wines are unashamedly traditional, perhaps showing considerable earthiness or even brett (see Wine Faults) while others have a piercing purity of fruit. A bready, autolytic NV Champagne from a grande marque contrasts in style to a more individual, barrel-aged, single variety, no-malo grower Champagne.

Not all wine is ageworthy; some are intended to be drunk young (which is what most consumers prefer to do). Not all wine *should be* complex or intellectual: a lot is simply for straightforward, affordable pleasure. A 'non-traditional' style might be one that stretches a grape or a regional expression to its limits: perhaps by testing the extremes of ripeness (one way or the other) or using unexpected ageing methods.

Finally, and importantly, there are no right or wrong wine styles (although we all have our preferences); there are only various degrees of success or failure within those styles. When assessing a wine, leave your prejudices aside to focus on how successful the wine is *within its style*.

Here are examples of terms appropriate for describing wine style, though there are many more: modern, traditional, ageworthy, (lavishly) oaked, mass-market, broad appeal, ambitious, complex, reliable, unusual, distinctive, subtle, intense, vibrant, earthy, dry, powerful, delicate.

Winemaking and method of production questions

The most logical way to approach questions which ask about how a wine was made is to consider every winemaking step in sequential order, from the time the grapes are harvested until the wine is in bottle. Not every point below will need noting for every wine, but your answer should be broken down into these kinds of smaller points. And if you proceed in sequential order through each moment in the winemaking process, you are less likely to miss anything. The most important thing is that every point you make *must be backed up with evidence from the glass*.

In the following list, the word 'probable' means that it is difficult/impossible to taste this in the glass, so the factor may be mentioned, but the 'probable' qualification should be attached, e.g., 'pump over probable.' And be aware that you may not receive a mark for this kind of observation.

GPF – MBMB is your mnemonic!

Grapes: you can discuss here which varieties are present, if relevant. E.g., if varieties have not been asked about already, or in the case of sparkling wines or other blends: 'Pinot Noir and Chardonnay grapes harvested…'. Then consider the condition of grapes at harvest: botrytis, frozen grapes, ripe/unripe (e.g. early harvest such as Hunter Valley Semillon or long hang time in Napa – provided you can justify from the glass). Whole bunches: certain styles such as sparkling wines/carbonic Beaujolais require harvesting whole bunches, so note that. (Although if you can taste stem inclusion, it is better to leave that observation until the fermentation stage of the answer.)

Pre-fermentation handling: could include preparation of dried grapes (Amarone, passito etc). Cold soak for reds is only a 'probable' because it is questionable whether you can perceive it. Skin contact for whites. Direct press is a 'probable' for pale coloured rosé.

Fermentation: consider vessel, temperature, method (e.g. charmat, halted fermentation in sweet/fortified wines); maceration technique for reds (carbonic maceration, stem inclusion; punch down/pumpover is only probable); duration of fermentation is a probable (e.g. classic Barolo reveals extended maceration).

Malolactic fermentation: for whites: state whether it has occurred or not (because it has been stopped or otherwise).

Blending: of varieties. Blending across parcels or vintages for freshness/richness/balance is likely to be only probable, because it is difficult to say with absolute confidence from evidence in the glass (the one exception may be NV Champagne, which can often be more autolytic than vintage).

Maturation: note vessel, duration, lees contact, anaerobic or oxidative ageing. There is plenty to say here for all wines, but especially for sparkling, sweet and fortified styles.

Bottling: filtration or not; you can also refer back to maturation length (e.g., 'early bottling for freshness') and time in bottle, which is very relevant for traditional method sparkling wines (do not forget about dosage either).

For questions that ask about quality with reference to winemaking techniques, the examiners are asking you to consider which elements in the winemaking process have most significantly affected quality. Do not repeat all the points above – you need to focus solely on the most relevant. These will vary strongly according to wine style. Some examples of winemaking that are important for defining the style and quality of the wine:

- Cool fermentation temperatures for crisp, aromatic wines like New Zealand Sauvignon Blanc
- Absence of malolactic fermentation in styles like Loire Chenin Blanc
- Halted fermentation for German Prädikat styles
- Time on lees for traditional method sparkling wines
- Length of time in barrel for traditional red styles, particularly for Reserva/Riserva levels in Italy and Spain
- Oxidative handling for Madeira, Oloroso and Rutherglen Muscat

Commercial appeal/potential/positioning questions

These varying terms all drive at the same thing: how should this wine be sold? Once again, breaking down your answer into a series of short points will ensure you cover all the ground.

<u>CSPO is your mnemonic!</u>

Channel: where would you sell this wine? What is the most appropriate sales channel? Break this answer down into two sub-sections: on-premise and off-premise. The best answers will give detailed suggestions rather than generic ones. E.g., rather than saying 'restaurants,' what kind of restaurant? Have a standard set of possible options, such as: 'family or chain restaurants,' 'fast casual,' 'mid-tier' or 'white tablecloth' or 'sommelier-led.' You can also specify cuisines where appropriate, or if the wine is very tied to the food of its country of origin, phrases such as 'in restaurants serving the cuisine of the country of origin.' Also do not forget other forms of on-premise such as wine bars, cinemas, hair salons etc.

For off-premise, consider what type of store would carry this wine. Some options: 'big box retail or supermarkets,' 'independent or specialist merchants,' 'fine wine merchants and auction houses.'

Segment: to whom should this wine be sold? What segment of consumers is best targeted? Once again, to answer this question successfully, you need a roster of consumer segments. Create your own, but some examples might include: 'weekday drinkers,' 'enthusiasts,' 'explorers/adventurous consumers,' 'price conscious,' 'confused/overwhelmed,' 'image seekers,' 'collectors.'

Price: what price band does this wine fit into? You need to have some standard price bands that are clearly defined both in your head and whenever you mention them. E.g., 'entry level' is below $/€10; 'mid-tier' is $10-20; then 'premium,' 'super premium' and 'luxury.' Or whatever terminology speaks to you. But when discussing price, mention both the band and the price. E.g., 'will sell for a mid-tier price ($10-20)…'

Other: what other factors will influence sales of this wine? Does the wine have a broad or narrow appeal? Are there many competitors? Is there any seasonality to sales?

If there are a large number of marks available for a commercial question, there is no harm in mentioning quality as a way of positioning the wine within the categories described above; just because it is not a quality question, there is no ban on mentioning it. In fact, doing so often facilitates answering the rest of the question well.

If the question asks about **wine style** in relation to commercial potential, focus particularly on the segment part of the answer – the style of the wine will determine the target consumer.

If the question asks about **winemaking** in relation to commercial potential, there is likely to be something noteworthy about the winemaking. In that case, think about the type of consumer who would enjoy this style or not, and thus via what channel the wine is best sold.

Appendix II: Table of Structure

White Variety	Shape of acidity	Type of acidity	Level of acidity
Chardonnay	Linear, horizontal	Firm, broad	Moderate
Riesling	Vertical	Steely	High
Chenin Blanc	Crescendo	Bracing	High
Pinot Gris	Linear, horizontal	Tingly, zesty, humming	Moderate
Sauvignon Blanc	Spherical	Prickly, unintegrated	High
Melon de Bourgogne	Supernova	Jagged, sharp	High
Aligoté	Spherical	Sharp, jagged	High
Gewürtztraminer	Ball/point	Soft	Low
Muscat	Linear	Firm	Moderate
Pinot Blanc	Linear	Bright	Moderate
Marsanne	Circle	Bright	Moderate
Viognier	Linear	Steely, bright	Moderate
Semillon	Linear, horizontal	Electric, buzzing, zesty	High
Grüner Veltliner	Rollercoaster	Tangy, humming, buzzing	High
Albariño	Wall to wall	Zesty, tart	High
Viura (Macabeo)	Diffuse	Soft, fruit-wrapped	Moderate
Verdejo	Linear	Zesty	Moderate
Vinho Verde varieties	Rinse, shower	Tart, prickly	High
Assyrtiko	Square	Powerful	High
Furmint	Shower, rinse	Prickly, zesty, popping	High
Torrontés	Linear	Firm, juicy	Moderate
Garganega	Linear	Consistent, steady	Moderate
Cortese	Linear	Zesty	Moderate

White Variety	Shape of acidity	Type of acidity	Level of acidity
Verdicchio	Linear	Steely	Moderate
Arneis	Linear	Firm	Moderate
Vermentino	Linear	Firm, zesty	High
Fiano	Linear	Steely	High
Greco	Expanding, radiating outwards	Zesty	Moderate

Red Variety	Location of tannin	Type of tannin	Level of tannin
Cabernet Sauvignon	Gums	Grippy, fine grained	High
Merlot	Gums	Grippy, grainy, clayey	Moderate
Pinot Noir	Tongue, roof of mouth	Silky, velvety, chalky	Moderate
Syrah	Tongue, gums	Powdery, chalky, velvety	Moderate
Grenache	Everywhere	Sticky, diffuse, gangly	Moderate
Cabernet Franc	Gums	Grippy, grainy	Moderate
Malbec	Gums, jaw	Grippy, grainy	High
Carmenère	Gums	Powerful, grainy	High
Gamay	Gums	Chalky	Moderate
Mourvèdre	Gums	Heavy, coarse	High
Carignan	Gums	Grainy	High
Tannat	Gums	Powerful, dry, dripping	High
Blaufränkisch	Gums, rear gums	Chalky, grainy	Moderate
Tempranillo	Cheeks	Chalky	Moderate
Mencia	Cheeks	Chalky	Moderate
Xinomavro	Rear gums	Grippy, grainy	Moderate
Saperavi	Gums	Sticky, grainy	Moderate
Touriga Nacional blends	Gums	Grippy	High
Zinfandel	Everywhere	Velvety, chewy, loose knit, diffuse	Moderate
Pinotage	Gums, cheeks	Powerful, coarse	High
Dolcetto	Gums	Grainy	Moderate
Barbera	Gums	Grainy, chalky	Moderate
Nebbiolo	Gums	Long grained, sandy	High
Corvina	Gums	Chalky, dusty	Moderate
Sangiovese	Gums	Sandy, grainy	Moderate
Montepulciano	Gums	Chalky, grainy	Moderate
Aglianico	Gums	Sandy, coarse	High

Red Variety	Location of tannin	Type of tannin	Level of tannin
Nero d'Avola	Gums, rear gums	Grainy, sandy	Moderate
Nerello Mascalese	Gums	Sandy, grainy	High
Primitivo	Gums	Chalky	Moderate
Negroamaro	Gums	Coarse, grippy	High

This table is a summary of the remarks at the beginning of every grape variety entry. This and the subsequent table are available for PDF download at vintagevariation.com/beyond-flavour

Appendix III:

Table of Indicative Analytical Values

This table is an attempt to record indicative levels of residual sugar and alcohol for important sparkling, sweet and fortified wine styles worldwide. Indicative means 'typical.'

The values I have included below come from reading many tech sheets for the wine styles in question. But apart from certain analytical details that are legally mandated (e.g. sugar levels in Champagne styles), there will always be exceptions to the figures listed below. For that reason, let me be clear about what I am claiming for the figures below: they are *what I would expect to find* in the named wine style. If a range is stated, it simply means there is insufficient commonality to be more precise.

Wine	Country and region	Sugar g/l	ABV	Notes
Rutherglen Muscat Classic	Australia, Victoria	200-280	17.5%	Grand and Rare styles have higher sugar levels: 270-400g/l
Ontario Riesling Ice Wine	Canada, Ontario	250	8-13%	
Alsace: Vendanges Tardives (VT)	France, Alsace	50-100	12-13%	
Alsace: Selection de Grains Nobles (SGN)	France, Alsace	150-300	10-12%	

Wine	Country and region	Sugar g/l	ABV	Notes
Sauternes/Barsac	France, Bordeaux	125-165	13-14%	
Champagne Brut Nature/Brut Zero	France, Champagne	0-3	12%	No dosage added
Champagne Extra Brut	France, Champagne	0-6	12%	
Champagne Brut	France, Champagne	<12	12%	
Champagne Extra Dry	France, Champagne	12-17	12%	
Champagne Sec	France, Champagne	17-32	12%	
Champagne Demi-Sec	France, Champagne	32-50	12%	
Champagne Doux	France, Champagne	50+	12%	
Bonnezeaux, Quarts de Chaume	France, Loire	125-250	12%	
Coteaux du Layon	France, Loire	80-120	11-12%	Minimum of 34g/l
Vouvray Sec	France, Loire	<10	12-14%	
Vouvray Demi Sec	France, Loire	10-30	12-14%	
Vouvray Moelleux	France, Loire	40-100	12-12.5%	
Vins Doux Naturels: Banyuls/Maury	France, Roussillon	90-100	16.5%	
Vins Doux Naturels: Muscat de Beaumes de Venise	France, Rhone	100-115	15%	
German Riesling Trocken	Germany, various regions	<9	11.5-13.5%	
Mosel Riesling Kabinett	Germany, Mosel	45	8.5%	
Mosel Riesling Spätlese	Germany, Mosel	60	8.5%	
Mosel Riesling Auslese	Germany, Mosel	90	8.5%	
Mosel Riesling Beerenauslese	Germany, Mosel	150	6.5%	
Mosel Riesling Trockenbeerenauslese	Germany, Mosel	250-400	6%	
Mosel Riesling Eiswein	Germany, Mosel	150	6.5%	
Tokaji Aszu 5 Puttonyos	Hungary, Tokaj	150-160	11%	4 puttonyos: 120-

Wine	Country and region	Sugar g/l	ABV	Notes
				150g/l; 6 puttonyos: 180g/l+
Lambrusco	Italy, Emilia Romagna	3-12	11-12%	Figures quoted are for Brut styles; dry, demi-sec, amabile or other similar styles will show higher levels of RS
Asti	Italy, Piedmont	80	7.5%	
Moscato d'Asti	Italy, Piedmont	115	5.5%	
Prosecco	Italy, Prosecco	15	11%	Drier and 12% for higher quality examples
Vin Santo	Italy, Tuscany	70-200	14-17%	
Amarone della Valpolicella	Italy, Veneto	<10	15-17%	
Recioto della Valpolicella	Italy, Veneto	50-120	11-15%	
Port (all types)	Portugal, Douro	90-110	20%	
Madeira: Rainwater (Tinta Negra)	Portugal, Madeira	50-80	18%	
Madeira: Sercial	Portugal, Madeira	40-60	19%	
Madeira: Verdelho	Portugal, Madeira	70-90	19%	
Madeira: Bual	Portugal, Madeira	90-100	19%	
Madeira: Malmsey	Portugal: Madeira	100-130	19%	
Sherry, Fino/Manzanilla	Spain, Jerez	0	15%	
Sherry, Amontillado/Palo Cortado	Spain, Jerez	0	17.5-19%	

Wine	Country and region	Sugar g/l	ABV	Notes
Sherry, Oloroso	Spain, Jerez	0	20%	Longer-aged examples will show higher alcohol
Sherry, Cream	Spain, Jerez	130	18%	Pale cream: 45-115g/l
Sherry, Pedro Ximinez	Spain, Jerez	400	17%	
White Zinfandel	USA	35	10-12%	

Acknowledgements

I am grateful to all reviewers, professional and non-, who took the time to record their thoughts on the first edition. Recommendations and critiques from these correspondents fuelled much of my desire to write a second, better, edition. I am grateful too to those who mentioned the book on social media; it is still a joy to me every time I get a message about the book on Instagram or elsewhere, from all around the world.

For the producer recommendations, where my tasting experience was insufficiently broad, I leaned on wine reviews on jancisrobinson.com and from the indispensable *Hugh Johnson's Pocket Wine Book*, 2020 edition.

To Jessica Green, who gave up a huge amount of her own time to give the manuscript of this book a thorough editing it very much needed. The book is so much better because of it and I am so grateful. To Chloe Lombard and Ashton Dunn, for the wonderful illustrations and for being so easy to work with.

To the many wine students who have been generous in their appreciation of the book and have given me many tips on further improvements — thank you and good luck with your studies! And most importantly, thanks to all those who have generously shared so many great wines with me. You are too numerous to list, but a special mention to my friend and neighbour Cory Lipoff, who is almost single-handedly responsible for my Burgundy knowledge. And finally, to my friends and family who have been unfailingly enthusiastic about the book, even when I have not always been. Thank you for your support!

Index

Sauvignon Blanc in, 52

stylistic norms, 181–182

Syrah, 111

unusual wine styles

tasting for origin, 175

V

Vacqueyras, 114

varietal characteristics tasting for
origin, 175

variety questions in blind tasting
exam questions, 191

velvety, diffuse type of tannin
Zinfandel, 135–136

Verdejo, 70

Verdicchio, 78–79

Vermentino, 80–81

vertical shape of acidity
Riesling, 36, 37

Vinho Verde, 71–72

Vino Nobile di Montepulciano
Sangiovese, 147

Vin Santo, 163, 167

Vins Doux Naturels (VDNs), 168

vintage questions in blind tasting
exam questions, 192

Viognier, 61–63

Viura (Macabeo), 68–69

volatile acidity, 24, 144, 179, 190

Volnay, 101

Vosne-Romanée, 100

Vougeot, 99–100

Vouvray, 44

W

wall to wall shape of acidity
Albariño, 67–68

Washington State
Cabernet Sauvignon, 91

White Burgundy, 32

white grape varieties, 30–83

Albariño, 67–68

Aligoté, 54–55

Assyrtiko, 72–73

Chardonnay, 30–35

Chenin Blanc, 42–45

Furmint, 73–74

Gewürztraminer, 55–57

Grüner Veltliner, 65–67

Marsanne, 60–61

Melon de Bourgogne
(Muscadet), 53–54

Muscat, 57–58

Pinot Blanc, 58–59

About the Author

Nick Jackson is a British Master of Wine and wine importer living in the US. His wine career started at the University of Cambridge, from where he received a Ph.D. in Theology. While there, he was a member of the Cambridge University Blind Wine Tasting Team that defeated Oxford in the annual blind tasting varsity match in 2011.

After Cambridge, Nick worked for Sotheby's Wine for seven years, in London and New York. He left Sotheby's at the end of 2018 and he now runs two businesses: Vintage Variation, a fine wine consultancy; and from 2022, Crescendo Wines, a fine wine importer serving Florida's restaurants and retailers.

Nick passed the WSET Diploma in 2014, began the Master of Wine study program in 2015, passed the theory and tasting exams at his first attempt in 2017, and became a Master of Wine in 2019. His research paper addressed wine in seventeenth century English poetry.

The first edition of *Beyond Flavour* was self-published in 2020 and received widespread praise in the wine media, with *Wine Spectator* calling it 'quietly the best wine book to come out in recent memory.'

Nick lives in Jupiter, Florida.

@nickjacksn

www.vintagevaration.com/beyond-flavour

Printed in Great Britain
by Amazon

26355907R00129